The Shortest Journey

The Shortest Journey

Sanna Suutari

Freedom from the shell

www.freedomfromtheshell.com

FIRST EDITION IN ENGLISH
Finnish original Maailman lyhyin matka

TRANSLATOR
Eeva-Liisa Pitkänen

COVER AND LAYOUT
COVER PHOTOGRAPH
Graphic Designer
Janne Paajanen
www.j8graphics.com

ISBN 978-952-69340-0-6 (PAPERBACK)
ISBN 978-952-69340-1-3 (PDF)

This book is based on a true story.
I dedicate it to You.

Table of Contents

PART THREE: FREE FROM THE SHELL

Foreword

I have never met Sanna Suutari before, so when she contacted me to write the foreword for her book, I admittedly had some doubts about writing it. Then, I started reading about her experiences and journey to Truth. Something in me shifted. There was no way I couldn't write the foreword! The inspiration behind the words was recognizable and spoke of Truth; the same Truth I recognized in the spiritual masterpiece, *A Course in Miracles*.

A Course in Miracles, a thought system I teach and adhere to is a purely non-dualistic thought system. It says there is only one reality that is true, and that is God, awareness of perfect oneness. This book also sticks to the message that the ego, which Sanna and her mysterious "friend" call the self, is an illusion and doesn't exist. The self is based on the belief in separation. When we learn to let go of the self, and that which we are identified with in this world, we no longer suffer. Suffering is an illusion. The self is what gives meaning to this world, but when we let go of the meanings we give things, we can finally see our "real" Self, one with Truth, God, Love.

I love the way Sanna talks to this mysterious "friend" that appeared to her to give her these deep messages. It's simple, straight-forward, and a very relaxed style of writing. The way Sanna asks questions are very relatable and probably the way most of us would ask questions when we are confronted with ideas that at first may seem shocking or alarming.

One doesn't really need to be an expert on spiritual teachings to let these ideas sink in, but I would say it requires an open mind, because this book asks you to look at yourself and question every value you think you hold, similar to *A Course in Miracles*. The material is presented in a non-threatening way, more matter of fact, simple and to the point. That's my kind of book!

I usually never stray away from pure non-dualism, and this book has the same kinds of undertones in the way it describes the illusory nature of the world and ultimately ourselves. There is a "real" Self beyond this illusion, and this Self has nothing to do with the false self we believe we are now. I am pleasantly surprised at the wisdom expressed in this book and how consistent it is in terms of the content. The reader will access deeper parts of themselves if they allow their minds to open to the fact that maybe the body, the personality, and the world is not at all what it seems to be. So what is it? Those answers can be found in this book, but also leaving something for you to discover for yourself.

I highly recommend this book to anyone wanting to look deeper into the nature of who you are, and to those who have always felt there was something more than this body, world and self we believe we are. Perhaps you even feel something is missing at times. This is also explained with clarity, and I would add that without God there is nothing. What you find may surprise you, but also be something you recognize and have always known in the depths of your being...the Truth about YOU. As you come to know the Truth, you will be known.

Cindy Lora-Renard, *author of A Course in Health and Well-Being, teacher of A Course in Miracles, and Spiritual Life Coach*

Acknowledgements

From the original Finnish edition.

Heartwarming thanks to Juha Kuvajainen and Päivi Piiroinen for all your help during the writing process. The support and guidance that I received has surely crossed all "traditional" conventions and ways of acting. Our co-operation has been rewarding and effortless.

Big thanks to my parents Maija and Markku, my sisters Mervi and Meeri as well as to all my friends for their understanding and patience which this "Sanna always just writes" process has required. Thank you also in general for all the support and understanding that I have received after the journey.

Warm thanks to Emilia whose open and interested attitude towards life always brings a smile to my face. Don't worry Emppu, you can read this book later when you have grown a little bit more.

Big thanks to the book's Jani for all the support and understanding that you have given both during and after our journey. Smilingly I follow your flight.

Heartwarming thanks to my husband, Luke, who "stopped me" and guided my attention bravely and gently but firmly towards the Truth. Thank you also for the support that I have received during the writing process, thank you for your understanding and patience.

I also want to thank all the people who have participated in this English edition.

A warm thanks to Eeva-Liisa Pitkänen and to Luke for a great job in helping me to translate the text. We all had our own parts in the process. Thank you for your willingness and a wonderful outcome. Big thanks also to Fiona Robertson for proof reading the text. You did a wonderful job too.

Warm thanks to Janne Paajanen for a beautiful cover and the layout of the book. Big thanks also for the openness of Cindy Lora-Renard in getting to know the text and making an inspiring foreword.

After all I am thanking, and at the same time summarizing, all the thanks to the one and same Source, Love, Self, which we all Are. Magnificent thanks to inner Voice, that lead me to realize who I really Am and which without this book wouldn't have born. Thank you Life for all your Love.

Sanna Suutari
2019

Preface

I want to tell the story of a woman called Sanna who believed she was born and would someday die, the story of my self.

When my self died I didn't know what was happening. I had always connected death with the body and when the disintegration of my self gradually began I didn't have any idea what it was all about. It was an extremely confusing time. I went through a process during which my feelings changed from one extreme to another, from complete joy to indescribable feelings of fear. I had no idea what awakening meant – in fact I had never heard anything about it before. I had no religious or spiritual background that could have helped me to understand what it was all about. I also wasn't interested in any kind of magic or other supernatural matters. Supernatural meant to me only the things that couldn't be proven through the five senses.

I want to tell you this story because each of us will go through the same process sooner or later. I don't mean that your experience would be exactly the same as mine; that is impossible. The way you experience your life originates from your self, and that is the reason why no-one else can have the same experience as you. I am telling this story to help you along your own path. You see, Love Loves you.

This story begins in Manjimup, a place located in south-western Australia, relatively close to Perth – relatively close because three hundred kilometers doesn't feel much by Australian standards. For me, this became a concrete experience as I sat in a van hour after hour for over seven months. I was realizing a dream of mine with the man I loved, a dream that included Australia, a retro van, surfboards and a guitar. We had been driving around Australia for thousands and thousands of kilometers before we landed in Manjimup.

We came to Manjimup because we needed work. We needed money to continue our journey to a new destination. Australia is full of fascinating places and we hadn't seen all of them yet. I really mean what I'm saying: I wanted to see and experience everything about Australia, just everything! I wanted to surf at beautiful beaches, snorkel and dive in the middle of a coral paradise, enjoy the magical sunsets, admire the giant red rock, make love with my man on a deserted beach under the stars. I wanted to pat the kangaroos and listen to the howls of wild dingos in the desert. I wanted to see Aboriginal villages and swim with the dolphins – of course in the clear turquoise-coloured water. I wanted to watch whales and look a giant crocodile in the eye. Most of my wishes had already come true but not all, not quite all.

I also felt I was getting a bit tired. Our dream wasn't only limited to Australia. Before landing in Australia, we had already wandered around south-eastern Asia backpacking for four months, trying to see and experience all that Asia had to offer. I was making my "once in a lifetime" dream come true, and didn't want to waste one second of it. I was deeply grateful to have been able to do something I really loved. Different, new things have always fascinated me. When you are travelling you have a chance to meet new people, admire exotic animals, try everything new and exciting and see endless kinds of beauty.

According to the original plan, the journey was supposed to last for about a year, but right before arriving in Manjimup we had decided to continue on for another five months. As I already mentioned we hadn't had the chance to experience everything in Australia yet, and New Zealand and Bali were still to come. Additionally, neither of us had any idea what we would do when we returned to Finland. This actually felt like quite a big problem, so the few months' extra time was more than relieving. Work and Holiday visas made it possible for us to earn money. Back in Finland we didn't have our own residence or permanent jobs to return to. We had gotten rid of them both before starting on this journey. The realization of my dream was far more important to me than an apartment of my own or my permanent job as a kindergarten teacher.

We had decided to work in Manjimup for two months, after which we would head for Sydney. I felt happy although I began to miss my family and friends a lot. The idea of one year apart from the people close to me had seemed impossible at first, but everything had gone well so far because luckily I was in the company of my beloved companion and safety net, Jani.

So this was my situation when it all began, a process that in hindsight received a big boost from the events that were to follow in Manjimup.

PART ONE

Imprisoned by the shell

1

You don't know who you really Are

— You don't know who you really Are. A calm male voice interrupted my thoughts.

I looked up. A man was standing right in front of me across the other side of the table. He was around forty years old. I had never met him before. He had uttered the words very calmly, with assurance, as if he had just stated something very obvious in passing. I noticed immediately that his voice was not in the least arrogant or scornful. The words were not meant to hurt or humiliate anyone. There was warmth in the voice.

I stared at the man with my mouth open. His dark brown eyes were looking straight into mine. The man spoke English, in a typical Australian way, and I came to the conclusion that he was a local resident, or perhaps he had already spent some time in Australia.

— Excuse me? I wanted to be sure I had heard right.

— You don't know who you really Are, the man said again calmly.

— I don't know who I am? I laughed with genuine embarrassment.

— Yes, the man answered calmly again and nodded his head as if giving more emphasis to the meaning of his words.

I didn't know what to think. I looked at him questioningly. I didn't know who I was? The thought seemed really strange to me. Of course I knew who I was. I was Sanna. I knew myself all right, it was quite clear. I could have been offended by his words, but as he did not sound defiant at all, I was just confused. The man clearly suggested that he had some kind of picture of me, and I couldn't understand how that was possible. I decided to ask him an insinuating question.

– Excuse me, but have we met before?

The man remained quiet and looked at me, smiling. There was something in his look, something really special. It was not a hungry man's hungry look; there was something much deeper, something that left me speechless. And the smile was very gentle too. An uneasy feeling spread over me and I was a little embarrassed. I didn't understand what the man wanted and why he didn't answer me.

Now, afterwards, I can say that the man really wanted nothing of me. He was just there, present and available for me only. Life had given me a chance, a gift I could not even have dreamed of.

I had spent the last few days alone. I had a lot to think about. Although we had decided to continue the trip, our future in Finland occupied my mind. I felt restless; I didn't know what I really expected from life. I began to suspect that the man had somehow been following me without my knowing, and instinctively noticed my mental state. Maybe he was worried about me.

– Excuse me, I don't exactly understand what you mean, I said. I'm quite all right. I only have a lot on my mind, but nothing serious. Thanks for your concern.

– I'm not concerned about you. You just don't know who you really Are, the man said gently again and didn't, in fact, seem to be concerned about me in the least.

I was at a loss again. I didn't understand what he meant, and sighed deeply.

– Unfortunately, I don't understand what you mean. I know very well who I am. I just have so many things to occupy my mind. My own personal things. Understand?

The man looked at me quietly for a while.

– Your own things. I understand that very well.

I was glad. I was hoping he would now leave me alone because I didn't feel like talking at all. I was tired and I wanted to be by myself. But the man didn't go anywhere, instead he sat down on the chair next to me. I sighed deeply again and would surely have stood up and left had I already finished eating. We were in the communal lunch area of a camping site. I decided to go on eating and behave as if he didn't exist at all.

I soon emptied my plate, got up and went to wash up my things. The man didn't budge, he just remained sitting on his seat quietly. I was getting annoyed, and regretted my behaviour a little. Maybe I had been too rude. I walked back to him.

– I'm sorry. I'm just a bit tired. I've had a very exhausting day but that's not your fault in any way. I'm sorry. I haven't even introduced myself. I'm Sanna. What's your name?

– You believe in the same illusion as millions of other people do. You identify yourself with your identity, the illusion called I.

– Excuse me? I blurted out. I was confused again.

– Since your birth you have been taught to believe that you are the same as your identity, the story woven around your name. So you believe in a mere story, a story about yourself, the man answered.

– What story? I looked at the man inquiringly again, because I didn't understand at all what he meant.

– I mean that you imagine you're Sanna, he said as if to explain an obvious misconception.

I didn't know what to think or reply, but I knew I was Sanna.

The man looked straight into my eyes, and there was really something special in his look. A nasty feeling of uneasiness spread over me again. I felt very uncomfortable, as if he had seen through me. I felt naked, clothed but still naked. No, that doesn't describe it either. His look pierced even deeper than that. It saw everything. I felt I was being X-rayed. I felt threatened.

– I'm not quite sure what you mean. I know I'm Sanna. Who do you think you are? Why don't you introduce yourself?

– I don't think anything about myself, the man answered, smiling again benevolently. I just know, without a shadow of doubt. I would tell you something about Myself but it is quite impossible to describe Me.

– OK, I laughed. There was clearly nothing wrong with the man's self-confidence. I felt a bit more relaxed.

– You are not Sanna either. You are something much more inconceivable. Actually, we are all One, and don't differ from each other in any way.

Now his story was getting really strange. I wondered whether the man was quite deranged or whether he was just making fun of me. But he seemed to be quite awake and in his senses. I examined him and tried to figure out what this all was about. As I didn't find any signs of mental disturbance in him, I started to suspect he was a member of some religious sect. Maybe he had been brainwashed by a group of fanatics. I was on the verge of leaving him alone but then I started to get worried. He might be in need of some help.

– You don't make sense to me. Do you need help? I asked him.

– You are running in a labyrinth you have built yourself, and you can't find the way out. You can't find the way out because you have built your labyrinth yourself and are in reality building it all the time.

– I'm in a labyrinth, I repeated. I hadn't got a clue what he was talking about.

– You want to find the way out, and you will find it. That is inevitable. But before you can find the way out, you have to realize how you are building your labyrinth.

– But I'm not building anything and I don't want out of anywhere. I just have things to think about. That's all there is to it, I tried to explain without actually knowing why.

– Oh yes. Your mind is the labyrinth.

I stared at the man quietly for a moment, trying to understand what he meant. My mind is a labyrinth? I had never before heard anything like that. My doubts were gradually dissipating and my interest was aroused. Maybe the man was a thinker, a kind of philosopher. He seemed quite harmless, at least.

– Do you mean that I am in my mind? I said with a timid laugh. – If I'm in a labyrinth and the labyrinth is my mind, then I should be in my own mind.

– That's it, right to the point. That's exactly the illusion you're living in.

– The illusion I'm living in? I don't understand. I shook my head in disbelief.

– You suppose you are alive.

I burst out laughing. That was quite an argument! The situation was becoming almost comical.

– I'm not supposing anything. I am alive! I raised my arms in the air and smiled happily. – And I'm really grateful for every single moment.

Although the last few days had been what they had been, that didn't mean I couldn't be grateful. I was living my dream. I knew I was lucky. Not everybody had the same opportunity. My thoughts about my own future were nothing compared with the famine in Africa. I had seen enough in my life to know I wanted to live my life to the full.

– You are grateful only for a first-class performance, the man stated bluntly.

– What performance? I'm talking about life, I clarified.

– That's right. Your performance can be happy or sad. After all it is of no matter, since it is only a performance. You identify yourself with the performance.

– What are you really trying to say?

– You create your life as long as you believe that you are living. It depends on you how you experience your life.

– Yes, sure. At least partly. It is my life that is in question. But there are other people in life too. The whole of life is not dependent on me, I said trying to understand what on earth the man was explaining.

– You don't see life as it Is. You see everything through a curtain you have sewn yourself. You are living in a mist and don't even know it. You can't know it since you are the mist yourself. There is nobody else in life.

– How come nobody else? You are here and I am here and everybody else. I felt really foolish.

– That's how you see the world because you imagine you are alive. You believe you are a separate individual with a body and personality of your own.

– Of course I am. I am me and you are you, I said emphatically, trying to state a self-evident truth.

– This I, I mean you, is an illusion. Nothing else. The illusion just feels true because you were born into it. You are an illusion yourself.

– Oh my! I'm no illusion, I'm here. I just don't seem to grasp what you're saying.

– You believe you're here because you identify yourself with your body. You believe you are your body. And naturally because you believe you are your body you regard as a truth everything that you experience through the medium of your body. This identification with your body is so evident that you are not even able to question it. Most people on this planet do not question this matter in any way. They identify themselves with their identities. The illusion feels true. It is true to you.

– So you think I'm not me? I said looking at the man questioningly.

– No, you're not. You are not you. You only think you are.

– I'm not me. I repeated the man's words aloud and tasted the thought at the same time in my mind: I am not I?

Crazy, totally senseless! I wasn't at all surprised that nobody questioned it.

2

You are not a body

– Your identity, I mean your idea of yourself, originates from your identification with your body. If you knew that you are not your body, you could no longer believe in your identity either, the man explained.

– But I do have a body. It's not that I believe I have it. I don't think you can suggest that you don't see my body right now?

– I'm not suggesting anything. I do see the body. It's only that you are not the body I See.

– Well, what do you think I am, then?

– Don't waste your time thinking about it. You would only stick to that idea and try to make it part of your identity, that is, yourself. You need something to identify yourself with to be able to preserve your own existence. Many people try for years to understand something that simply can't be understood through thinking. It's more important for you to concentrate on what you are not. Before you are able to know what you Are, you have to know what you aren't.

That explanation sounded very strange to me. I really had no idea what he meant. How could I understand anything without thinking and comprehending? Then, all of a sudden, I understood or thought I understood what he meant. Perhaps he was talking about life after death. Maybe he believed in the existence of the soul. Without even realizing it, I formed in my mind an idea of a soul I could identify myself with.

– Are you talking about the soul now? I asked hopefully.

– What do you mean by the soul?

– Well, I'm not quite sure. I know that some people believe they are actually an invisible figure or shape that continues the journey after death.

– How about you? Do you believe in it?

– I've never actually thought about it properly. And I don't even know whether that makes any difference. Here I am anyway, alive. What happens after death will become clear when we are dead, I answered truthfully.

– When you say death, do you mean the decomposition of the body? the man inquired.

– The decomposition of my body? I wasn't quite sure what he meant.

– When the heart stops beating and respiration ends, the body gradually begins to decompose and take another shape. That is what happens to all forms in this illusion that you call life. The whole illusion is pure energy that continuously changes form. Everything that is part of this illusion comes and goes. Nothing imagined is permanent. However, what you really Are never dies. It cannot die because It has never been born.

I didn't understand again what the man meant. I was at a loss, but that was not news to me any more.

– So you do believe in the soul? I tried to make him admit something at least.

– I think you are talking about the astral body now. The astral body is part of the illusion, and because the illusion does not exist, the astral body does not exist either. Still, I don't mean that leaving the body, for example, couldn't feel real to some people. All experiences are real to the person that experiences them. It is, however, important to realize that identification with the astral body is basically the same thing as the identification with the physical body. They both originate in the illusion that somebody or something really exists.

– What on earth are you saying?

– Some people tend to be in connection with forms living on other levels. Different experiences create an illusion and sometimes they may be connected with different levels. But what you really Are has nothing to do with any level or with any form living on any level.

I had no experiences of any kind of different levels or shapes living on different levels. To tell the truth, I wasn't particularly interested in anything like that. I decided, however, to be polite and continue the conversation.

– So, you believe that there is some other kind of life here apart from what we can see?

– As I said, the illusion is composed of different levels. The level you call life is observed through the senses. For you, obviously everything you can observe by hearing, smelling, tasting, feeling and seeing is true. Am I right?

– Yes. I don't believe in any supernatural creatures.

– Is everything that can't be experienced through the senses supernatural to you?

– I guess so. I'm not really a believer of any kind.

I had never considered myself a very gullible person but, on the other hand, I had never really pondered what believing actually meant. I had always taken certain things more or less for granted without actually thinking whether they were merely my beliefs or real facts.

3

Don't believe, find out

– What do you mean by believing? The man asked, referring to what I had just said.

– Believing is believing. That you believe in something you can't necessarily prove.

– And proving probably refers to some experience of yours? He looked at me again questioningly.

– Yes, or something that can be reasonably explained. I feel that people are gullible, they believe in things too easily.

– What do you mean when you say too easily?

I remained silent for a while and tried to think.

– I mean everything you can't be certain about.

– And you can be certain about your own experiences?

– Yes, I nodded approvingly.

– What about reason then? You just said that you consider certain or true everything you experience yourself or everything that can be reasonably explained. What do you mean by reason?

I had to spend a while again pondering this question.

– Reason is reasonable knowledge, I mean knowledge that has been proven true.

– Who proves it is true?

– A scientist or an expert, for instance.

– So you believe in what the experts say?

– Yes, I nodded vigorously.

– So you believe too, the man stated, looking straight into my eyes.

I remained silent for a moment. I didn't know what to say. I felt I was getting irritated and wondered whether that was exactly how he wanted me to react. Believing scientists and experts wasn't at all the same as believing in some vague new trend or idea. I took a deep breath.

– Well, maybe so. But that is a different sort of believing.

– Different sort of believing! The man said, smiling at me gently. – There are no different sorts of believing: you either believe in something or you don't. What you believe in is true for you and what somebody else believes in is true for them. For both one's own belief is true. You might say that believing has its levels, but these levels are ultimately insignificant because believing is always believing.

– How come?

– What you think is true is not necessarily true to someone else. And vice versa. What is true to someone else is not necessarily true to you. In other words, what is true to you is true to only yourself. And what is true to someone else is true to that person only.

– Well, that goes without saying, of course.

– Really? If you both have your own truths, then which truth is true?

Again, I had to think awhile about what he had said. I had never thought of it from that point of view. What kind of truth is the truth that is true to one person but not true to another?

– Everybody's own truth is based on their own experiences. You are full of thoughts that you think are true. Some of these thoughts are so deeply rooted in you that you just can't see through them. You have formed opinions for yourself, truths that may be nearly impossible for you to break. In this way, you may cling to and at the same time identify yourself with these thoughts so firmly that breaking this tie will succeed only when your self dies and your truth dissolves. You are like a spider spinning its web and looking at its own truth through the web. The illusion is full of thoughts; the illusion is a thought.

– But people should be free to think as they please! I exclaimed indignantly.

– Sure, they are – and there's nothing wrong with opinions. I'm just asking you to examine where your opinions come from.

– Well, an opinion is just an opinion. All opinions come from the people themselves.

– Exactly, from themselves. And what are opinions, if you are only an illusion yourself?

– I don't think that I am any kind of illusion myself, I answered firmly.

– I am not talking to you in order to persuade you to believe in some new idea or concept. I don't really want you to cling to yet another new idea which you could then lean on. I'm talking to you only to make it easier for you to let go of the rest of your beliefs.

– So you believe that I believe, I tried.

– I don't believe, I know. I know because without you there would be no one who believes.

– I'm not exactly sure what you mean. You really couldn't make me believe in anything even if you tried. I've seen what religions and different beliefs can do, and I know for sure that none of them is for me.

I felt my pulse rise. In my opinion, various religions and believing in general were often causing more harm than good on this planet. Converting by force and the controversies between different religions were pure insanity to me. (I did not understand yet what the man meant, so I reflected his message into my own opinions.)

– Believing is not connected only with different religions. It covers everything that is true to yourself.

I was astonished.

– Do you really mean that everything I believe in is not really true?

– Yes.

– Is everything you believe in true then?

– I don't believe.

– Oh yes, that's true. You know, I said with a little bit of doubt. – What if you believe you know?

– When you know there's no one who knows. And when there's
no one who knows, there can be no one who believes he knows.

– Yeah, right. That's really clear.

– In order to burst the illusion you have to question everything you
believe in, everything you have learned and everything that is true
to you.

I didn't say anything, I just stared at the man. I didn't understand
what he meant by the illusion or anything he was saying. I couldn't
have imagined then, what a fundamental change I was involved in.
If I had had even a hunch of what he was trying to say, I would almost certainly have questioned the change itself. I know now that
everything is possible. There are no limits in life. All limits are only
in your imagination. You set the limits for yourself.

4

Openness

The man remained silent for a moment, as if pondering what kind of words he would choose for me.

– Questioning is important, but it is just as important to be open. As I already said, I don't want you to believe me. You have to find out for yourself, that's the only way. And when you are finding things out for yourself, don't let your doubts block the way. When I say questioning, I'm not talking about an attitude behind which you can hide. Your only obstacles are your own doubts.

– I agree. That's why I'm listening to you.

I instinctively knew that the man was trying to make me see something important. I could have walked away leaving him sitting there alone, and at the start I almost did so, but luckily something inside me made me stay. I was curious by nature and everything new and different fascinated me. I didn't understand at the time how important it was for me to be so open-minded. If I had remained in the shadow of my own doubts I could never have realized – or known as the man said – what I would later realize. Openness was one of my most important characteristics and helped me to proceed on the road which I had no idea about at the time. It's not the question of who hears, but who listens.

5

The Voice inside

– All your decisions are based either on love or fear, the man stated calmly.

– On love or fear? I looked at the man doubtfully for a moment. Life can't be so black and white?

– You consider this thought black and white because you don't actually know what love Is and where fear comes from.

– I think I have some kind of picture of love in my mind. Neither is fear a totally unknown concept to me. I was a little offended. Love was the most important thing in my life. I didn't yet know that Love is no thing.

– Do you know what Intuition or Instinct is? The man asked all of a sudden.

– The birds fly south because their instinct tells them to. Is that what you mean?

– Instinct is a Voice inside you. It keeps whispering to you all the time.

– Nobody is whispering anything to me, fortunately, I said with a laugh. – And I wouldn't even want to hear any extra voices. Do you hear them? I looked at the man, my eyes wide with wonder.

– Instinct can be heard but there is nobody any more who listens.

– I see, I said briefly because I didn't know what else to say.

– You don't hear the Voice inside you because either you don't hear It or you don't want to listen to It. In either case you hide the Voice yourself.

– Me, myself? I'm covering up the voice? Now I really don't understand what you mean. And why on earth would I even want to hear an extra voice?

– Right now, you are trying to hide the Instinct. It is not an extra voice. You just imagine that it is a separate voice because all your experiences are based on separateness. The Instinct is what Is. The Voice inside is whispering to you in many different ways, and the important thing is that only you know how the Voice communicates with you. The Instinct sends you messages – or better still, hints – into the illusion of the mind into your life.

As I realized later on there is no "extra voice" although it could very well be described as a Voice, the Voice of your heart. Love is whispering to you, often in surprising connections: in the eyes of an infant, in the morning paper or in a song that you hear on the radio. The feeling can at first be really startling, making you shiver all over. This is because you become aware of the Voice that you have always tried your best to hide.

– Are you saying that I get some kind of hints all the time?

– Yes, but you don't notice them because you don't want to notice them. The Instinct helps you to break the illusion but your self doesn't want that to happen.

– I don't want to break the illusion?

– By no means. You want to exist, by fair means or foul, no matter what. In fact, you do everything in your power not to hear or listen to the Instinct. You've even developed mighty defense forces to protect you.

– We-e-ll. I didn't really know what to say. I had never before heard of any kind of inner voice or defense forces.

– The defense forces are composed of different kinds of means that you use to preserve the illusion. These forces could be called guards as well. You have created them to stand guard at your door because you feel threatened. With the help of these guards you defend yourself. You use these defense forces without being aware of it yourself. You have built yourself a security wall that keeps you an unconscious prisoner.

I just sat there speechless, trying to catch the meaning of his words.

– You are walking in a labyrinth and can't find the way out. You have built walls that you feel keep you safe, and you are maintaining them all the time, even right now. You want to lean on your walls because walking in the labyrinth is exhausting. But the walls never stay up; they keep breaking down, over and over again. When one wall tumbles down you immediately build another one to take its place. Then you make yourself believe that you are safe once more. You're totally exhausted, dead on your feet, but still in continuous motion. You try and try without being able to stop, for stopping is impossible for you. Stopping is simply too much for you. You feel lost because you don't really want to be in the labyrinth but neither do you seriously want to find the way out either.

I was still sitting there without saying a word.

– The Voice inside you is not walking in a labyrinth. The Voice is flying Freely without a self.

The Voice inside is flying Freely. The self is not the inner Voice. The labyrinth is my mind. I was turning these sentences over and over in my head.

– You're listening either to your self or the inner Voice. Every time you listen to your self, the web you weave tightens, and every time you listen to the inner Voice, the web loosens. You can see life as it really Is only when your web dissolves.

– Oh yes. I am really like a spider spinning its own web, I said quietly, trying to remember what the man had said earlier.

– Yes, you are, or you are a person running in the labyrinth. They are both actually describing the same thing.

– So, I don't see life as it is because I'm running in the labyrinth and spinning a web? And then, of course, there are the defense forces as well? I wondered, scratching my head.

– Exactly. These are only symbols but they are sometimes very helpful.

I remained silent, trying to understand.

– The inner Voice can only be heard now, in this moment. It often appears as a presentiment that can't be explained. But, as you know, you don't like anything that can't be explained, so you either push the sentiment aside or start to analyse it, saying to yourself: "Should I?" or "I don't think I should." You don't trust the Instinct, you only trust yourself. You want to control your own life as well as the lives of others; you want to pull the strings. You want to preserve your own existence.

6

Confidence

The man's words about the inner Voice and about the fact that I was trying to control my own life as well as the lives of others too – which should not be done – seemed strange, to say the least. Of course, I had been accustomed to think, like so many other people, that I am responsible for my own life and that I, more or less, decide for myself which direction to take. I had embarked on this journey of my own free will and because I wished to.

– I'm at a loss again. There can't be anything wrong in a person's will to plan his or her own life? I asked, baffled.

– No, of course not. It is only important to recognize the source that has the need to plan. Your existence is based on control: you try to control everything and everyone. This controlling keeps your self alive. You rally your defense forces to help you not to lose control, even if you don't realize it yourself. You doubt and belittle, deny and argue, explain, dominate and complain – you will do anything to defend yourself. You might even develop a fear in order to keep a firm hold of your life. Fear is a splendid way to keep you on the leash. When you are afraid, you only listen to yourself, nothing else. Your self will do anything to keep the inner Voice out of your life.

I didn't say anything. I just listened.

– What if it wasn't you who decides about your life? What if you just listened only and solely to the inner Voice?

– But I don't even know what the Voice is, I answered truthfully. I didn't even believe yet that such a Voice existed. To me it sounded only like an interesting theory.

– One might sometimes listen to the Voice without realizing it and make it part of one's own identity. In that case, one thinks the Voice is part of oneself. This is a very cunning ruse of the self to make use of the Voice. But the Voice has nothing to do with the self. There is no Voice of one's own, there is only the Voice.

I looked at the man, still without uttering a word.

– Now when you know that the Voice exists, It gets louder and louder. You become more and more aware of It, and can't deny its existence any more, not consciously at least. It's now on the table, right in front of you. The man looked me in the eyes. – You choose which one you listen to, your self or the Voice. You are free to choose.

I stared at him flabbergasted. He seemed to be very sure that I knew what it was all about.

– I'm terribly sorry but I don't really know what you mean, I said honestly.

– Just trust Life and don't listen to your self, the man said with a smile.

At that moment, the door opened and I heard a very familiar voice say,

– Hey!

– Hello, honey, I answered happily. Jani, my partner and travelling companion, was walking towards me.

– I just came to see why you stayed behind.

– Oh, I'm stuck here in the kitchen, I answered with a smile.

– We're going downtown with Peter. Wanna come?

– Ah well, why not? I mumbled.

– OK, let's go then. Peter is waiting in the car.

– I just want to introduce someone to you. I pointed at the man. – This is... I looked at the man smiling because I couldn't finish my sentence. – Could I call you the Inconceivable, as you can't be described in words?

– You can call me whatever you like, he said smiling back at me.

Jani was gaping at both of us with eyes like saucers.

– Well, this Mr. Inconceivable is a fascinating fellow! We've had a really interesting conversation, I said, looking in his direction.

– I see. Glad to meet you. I'm Jani. Have you been here long?

– I'm not anywhere, the man answered calmly.

– Ahh, you're high? Jani was smiling questioningly.

– Yes, eternally high, the man said with a warm laugh.

– Hey, maybe we should leave now, it's better to talk to this man when you have more time, I suggested hastily.

Jani shrugged his shoulders. – OK, Off we go then.

– Thank you, it was nice talking to you. I'm sorry I was a bit rude at first, I said humbly to the man.

– You don't have to apologize for anything. You have done nothing wrong. Let's continue the conversation later on, the man said, still smiling gently.

– Are you staying at this campsite for long? I asked.

– Don't worry about that. Just trust Life.

– OK, I laughed and took Jani by hand. Together we walked towards the door.

– That man was really interesting, I said to Jani when we had gotten out of the kitchen. You will never guess what he said first.

– Well, probably asked your name, I guess, and where you're from, how long you've been travelling and what you do for work...

– Oh no, I interrupted Jani in mid-sentence. – Those are exactly the things that everybody asks us. And they are the things that we always ask them. But before I could even take a closer look at him, this man said to me that I don't really know who I am. See?

– No-o. Jani glanced at me a little confused.

– All that time when we were talking he didn't want to know one thing about me, and he didn't seem cold or indifferent.

– Well, you see, everybody is not so interested in you, Jani retorted.

– I know. And they don't have to be. He was just so totally convinced that I'm not really Sanna. And then he was talking about some kind of voice...

– Perhaps he was mixing you up with somebody else.

– No, he wasn't, you don't understand. But it doesn't matter. Forget the whole thing. You have to talk to him yourself.

We got to the van and jumped in like so many times before. Peter was sitting on the front seat. He was German and worked in Manjimup like us. Once the van started my thoughts flew from the conversation with the man to travelling and cutting apple trees. We all had the same job and travelling was our passion. It wasn't until bedtime that my thoughts returned to the conversation I had had with the man earlier. I tried to think about what he had meant. My thoughts revolved around the labyrinth and the Voice that was supposed to exist. I smiled to myself thinking of the man. He was a really peculiar case, and I hoped to meet him again sometime soon.

7

You are not your thoughts

A few days passed before I met the man again. I hadn't given much thought to our conversation after the first evening. My mind was occupied elsewhere. The working days had been long, and when I came back to the campsite I just crawled almost immediately into our van to rest. I was more and more tired every day and was becoming a real house mouse. The van felt like home as we had already been living in it for nearly seven months. I would have curled up on our rubber mattress once more, had I not seen the man again.

– Hi, Sanna. Do you have a minute?

– Oh, hello. Why?

– I'd like to show you something. I have a surprise for you.

– Ah, a real surprise! I said with a broad smile.

– Come with me. The man started walking straight on.

– Is it far? I tried to ask.

– Just follow me. Trust Life, the man said with a laugh.

We walked to a big tree nearby.

– Sit down here by me. The man pointed at the grass. I did what he asked me to do.

– Close your eyes and don't move.

This time I looked at him curiously, and didn't keep my mouth shut as usual.

– Weren't you supposed to show me something?

– Don't worry. I'll show you something all right. Just close your eyes now and don't say anything.

For some strange reason I trusted him completely and did what he had asked me to do.

– I'll tell you when you can open your eyes and move.

I nodded at him and sat down comfortably. I closed my eyes and tried not to move. A couple of seconds went by until I opened my eyes.

– How long do I have to sit here?

– Until I tell you. And if you open your eyes once again I won't be able to show you what I promised. Concentrate on your breathing now.

I sighed deeply and closed my eyes again. I really wanted to see what the man had promised to show me. I felt it had to be something important. This was the beginning of the most revolutionary experience of my life. I had made a parachute jump a couple of months earlier, but that was nothing compared to this experience. I remember how my thoughts literally jumped down on me the moment I closed my eyes. I had never before tried meditation, and didn't even know what it was. I had no idea what I had gotten myself into, but it soon became quite clear to me.

I sat there and the thoughts began to roll on at their own pace. Now, I only have to concentrate on my breathing, I thought to myself. I-in and o-out, i-in and o-out. Help! How long do I have to sit here after all? This is insane. It'll be quite cold soon, and I have to go and lie down. O-oh! I-in and o-out. This affects my lungs somehow, and my feet feel heavy. I-in and o-out, i-in and o-out. Jani will surely get worried soon. He doesn't have any idea where I am. I-in and o-out, i-in and o-out. I wonder what kind of working day tomorrow will be. Luckily it's Friday, two nights and then we'll have a day off. What luck! But of course, it's a good thing that we can work six days a week. We can really earn the money. You can always push hard for a couple of months. O-ohh! I-in and o-out, i-in and o-out. This makes no sense. Does he think I'm really stupid? What should I do? I could open my eyes, but then I won't see the surprise. It's got to be something really important. Otherwise he wouldn't make me sit here waiting. I-in and o-out, i-in and o-out. I wonder whether he is there at all any more. Should I open my eyes after all? No! Then I won't see the surprise. But this is quite crazy. I can't possibly concentrate on my breathing in this noise. I-in, o-out...

Time passed and more time passed. I felt I had been sitting still for an eternity, when I heard the man's voice at last.

– Just open your eyes.

– Aaah! What was all this about? I looked at the man totally exhausted.

– I wanted to show you your labyrinth.

– Was that the surprise? I felt disappointed.

– What did it look like in your labyrinth? He didn't seem to mind my indignation.

– I don't know. I wasn't able to concentrate, I said after a while. – My thoughts... It was really difficult to sit still, especially with my eyes closed.

– Some people voluntarily sit like that for hours, even days.

– That's awful. Why would anyone do that? I was shocked.

– For different reasons. But it is a good question.

– I don't understand why one would voluntarily want to torture oneself in that way. I shook my head. The experience had really been harassing to me.

– You had a chance to see your labyrinth, the man said smiling.

I was quiet and pondered what had happened.

– You are walking in your labyrinth right now. Through this experience I just wanted to bring your labyrinth right in front of your own eyes.

– Are my thoughts the labyrinth? Is that it?

– Yes. The thoughts you identify yourself with. I'm talking about your self. By stopping physically you have a chance to observe better who or what keeps you on a leash.

– I don't get it.

– At this moment you are a slave, a slave of your self.

– I'm the slave of myself? How could I be a slave of myself?

– You believe everything you say to yourself. You listen to yourself and act accordingly, like a puppet on a string. Your body is the puppet and your mind, I mean you yourself, is the person moving the puppet.

– But of course I listen to myself. That goes without saying. Who else should I listen to?

– That's right. It's completely clear to you because you identify yourself with your self. You regard your own thoughts as the truth. When you stopped physically you had a chance to see what you are following. The body generally follows your self and does exactly what it wants. What happened when you didn't do anything physically?

– I don't understand. I just thought.

– That's it. Your thoughts continued the motion, and this is the motion the body generally follows. You don't even notice how you physically follow your thoughts if you don't stop totally. You have the need to do something all the time. Even when you are still you feel you are doing something. You say: "Now I just am." But even just being is doing something for you. Do you understand?

– Probably not.

– Your self preserves its existence by doing. The man looked at me firmly. – Close your eyes again and follow your thoughts. Can you just let the thoughts come and go freely?

I closed my eyes and quickly opened them again. – I don't understand exactly what you want me to understand.

– Do you need yourself for thoughts to come and go freely in "your" mind?

I followed my thoughts for a while. – I don't know. I think I can't do anything without myself.

– Do you have to do something to breathe?

I observed my breathing for a while. – No, I don't have to do anything. The air goes in and out without my thinking about it.

– And the heart beats without you? The man looked at me questioningly.

– Yes, I admit that the heart beats without me having to do anything about it. But I still don't understand what you mean. There would actually be no heart or no need to breathe if there was no me.

– You're talking about the needs of the body now. Your body needs a heart and air to survive but you don't. You are not the body.

I smiled at the man. I thought I certainly had a body, I was my body.

– Your thoughts are jumping from one thing to another now, aren't they? The man looked at me with compassion. He seemed very patient, not nervous at all, although I didn't understand a word of what he was saying.

– Yeah, they are, I admitted with a nod. That was really true. I had so much to think about.

– Your thoughts are constantly moving back and forth between the past and the future. By concentrating on this moment, on now, you could see the surprise I promised.

– Oh, suddenly you're talking about surprises again! Weren't you supposed to show me one? I looked at the man with a wry smile.

– I don't think I told you when you would see the surprise. The man smiled back.

– Yeeaah right! I laughed joyfully. Well, what am I supposed to do next?

– You don't have to do anything, nothing at all. You see, this need to do something to get to the Destination is only a thought, very common, but still only a thought after all. The self uses this thought to preserve its own existence. But this is something we have already talked about.

– Again, I don't understand. You just said I have to concentrate on something.

– No, you don't have to, you can just Be. You can let the thoughts come and go without paying any attention to them. You don't have to listen to yourself.

– But I have to think to be able to act. I can't just be. I've got to go to work, for instance.

– It's for exactly this reason that I suggested you concentrate on the present moment, the now-moment. If you could just Be, you would understand that you have no need to concentrate or do anything at all to be able to see the surprise. This sounds very confusing because your self can't just Be. It's totally impossible. What you Are does not try to do anything and does not do anything either. On the other hand, It doesn't try not to do anything or isn't without doing. Being is the Background of doing and not doing. It just Is.

– Sorry? I lost the thread again, I said, looking at him at a loss.

– Don't worry. Just trust Life. Just let matters take their own course.

– You seem to have a great trust in life.

– Greater than you think, the man said, smiling again gently.

– I do admit that I have a tendency to worry too much sometimes. It might not be such a bad idea to just leave things alone. Right now, anyway, I can't do anything about my problems, I sighed.

– Just let the thoughts come and go.

– I'm not sure whether I'll be able to do that. It seems quite impossible.

– Your mind will calm down when there is nobody who thinks any more.

– Yes, sure, I laughed. – At that point there will probably be no worries to think about either.

– You won't die when your thoughts stop. You are not the continuum of the thoughts in your mind. You are not a person who clings to one thought after the another. You are not a self that lives through thoughts. You Are something much more wonderful.

I didn't say anything.

– When there is nobody who tries to think, the thoughts just come and go. What you really Are can be found behind the thoughts.

– Sounds interesting but we do have to think, after all. You have to think too, otherwise you wouldn't be able to talk with me!

– It's quite true that thoughts appear in the mind. I know, however, that I'm not my thoughts. There's nothing wrong with the thoughts. You don't have to stop thinking. It's quite enough if you just observe what there is between and behind the thoughts. Thoughts are just like the weather conditions in the sky; they come and go, if they are allowed to. When there is nobody who tries to cling to them, stop them or expect certain weather conditions, there is no one to suffer from them. Even if the sun doesn't always shine, the sky does not care. The sky just Is.

What the man said aroused my interest, and with each passing moment, I wanted more and more deeply to know what his words really meant. He was obviously trying to make me understand something I had never known how to think about before. And how on earth could I even think about it, because the very thinking seemed to be the obstacle that prevented me from understanding.

8

You are not your feelings

– Just a minute. How come thoughts just come and go? I've always thought it's me who thinks. Can you explain this a bit more exactly?

– Maybe you'll understand better if I use feelings as an example. A feeling always originates in a thought, if it isn't a spontaneous reaction to a stimulus. When I say stimulus I'm not talking about a thought. What you think you feel. Can you understand this?

– Yes, I can. Certain thoughts produce certain feelings. For example, when I think of my family and friends I feel melancholy because I miss them. And when I think of the sunset together with Jani I feel happy.

– That's it, exactly. Different thoughts create different feelings in your body. So, in practice, you decide yourself what you feel.

I looked at the man without saying anything because I wasn't quite sure what he meant.

– You have given a meaning to your thoughts, and these meanings are reflected in your body as sensations. What you think you feel.

– What are you trying to say?

– I'm saying that you are suffering because of yourself. All suffering originates in thoughts which have a meaning that causes suffering. The meanings are reflected as feelings in your body. You simply couldn't suffer if you didn't listen to yourself.

– Slow down. I can't keep up with you.

– Time after time, we come back to the illusion that you think you are. It's your self who keeps yourself alive through feelings. You believe you are a body that has feelings, so you identify yourself with these feelings.

– Yeah, it's true that I feel, I said to the man with a smile.

– If you could just let every feeling in your body come and go, you would recognise what is under them. In other words, if you could let all the feelings just be as they are without interfering in the process, you could perceive what you really Are.

I was lost for words again, and looked at the man quite confused.

– This is very challenging, because you are doing all you can to preserve your existence with the help of feelings. You take advantage of the feelings, you cling to them, you cover and deny them. You do anything it takes.

– What do you mean?

– You use your feelings as part of your identity. The question "how are you?" comes from the illusion, according to which there really is someone who is fine or something else, someone who feels something. You answer this question: "I'm feeling this or I'm feeling that". depending on how you feel at that particular moment. The feeling may just be transitory and you say: "I've been in a good mood today". Or the feeling may be frequent or more or less permanent. In this case it is called a characteristic, or even an illness. You might say: "I'm a cheerful person" or "I'm depressed". Using thoughts you develop a condition, a certain feeling that you can identify yourself with. What you think you feel.

– But an illness is not a thought. When you're ill you really feel it. Depression or cancer is no illusion.

– Illness always originates in thoughts. When you don't let all the thoughts, and at the same time the feelings, appear in the way they do, your body starts to react. You have either clung to some thoughts yourself, denied them or tried to cover them, very often without being aware of it. The self does not care about the well-being of the body, it only wants to preserve its own existence.

– What on earth do you mean?

– The self causes the illness.

– But nobody wants to suffer intentionally.

– The self will do anything to preserve its existence. It may even destroy the body in order to survive. The self doesn't Love you.

– I'm a bit confused. You are talking about the self as if it was something that is separate from me.

– The self doesn't have anything to do with what you really Are. The self is only an illusion that wants to preserve its existence at any price.

I rubbed my forehead for a moment. – I'm gradually getting really interested in what you mean by the self. There seems to be something to this.

– Splendid! This is a big step, if you really mean what you're saying, the man said encouragingly.

– I'm not so sure what I mean. There is something in your words that grabs me.

– Don't let that bother you. Just listen to me.

– Well. I'll try. I looked at him amused.

– Let's go back to feelings. You take advantage of your feelings by covering them, for example. By doing so, you don't consciously want to face an unpleasant feeling or thought in the present moment. You may, for example, express a feeling you don't actually feel at all. That's very common. Or you might numb the feeling you are hiding by drinking alcohol, medicating or taking drugs. Furthermore, feelings may be hidden behind an excessive need to exercise or eat. A continuous need to buy something or to have sex, constantly watching television or surfing the internet – these may also be ways to avoid a certain feeling and at the same time hide it. The need to do something all the time, anything, often comes from the same source, the need to cover. There are innumerable ways to do this. Anything goes as long as the hidden feeling does not rise to the surface.

– Yeah, people have many kinds of traumas, I said, just to say something.

– Traumas are thoughts, memories of experiences that have a meaning which produces suffering, and which one doesn't want to face in the present moment. And you don't even have to talk of traumas, everyone is always hiding something.

– That's true, I sighed.

– There's nothing wrong in hiding. It's enough just to become aware of what one is hiding. All feelings have to be faced in this moment, the now-moment. Otherwise you wouldn't know what you really Are. The self is a master of hiding, otherwise it wouldn't even exist. The self might also cover a certain feeling without realizing that it does so. Then we are talking about denial of the feeling. It's for this very reason that all traumas are born. One may have had such an unpleasant experience that one doesn't necessarily even remember what it was, but the experience stays in the background and affects the person without him or her being aware of it at all. This unconscious covering is possible with the help of the defense forces. Remember?

– Maybe. I have the need to control and command. Do the defense forces have anything to do with that?

– Yes. By controlling everything you want to hold the reins in your hands in all situations. You use the defense forces whenever you feel threatened. You have the need to defend yourself. Denial is the most radical way to defend oneself. You're defending yourself in other ways too, by rejecting, explaining, submitting, subduing, belittling, rationalizing and so on. You don't want to face an unpleasant feeling or the situation which gave rise to the feeling. You don't want to face the unpleasant feeling in the present moment.

I looked at the man, trying to weigh his words in my mind.

– Then there's one more way – I'll talk about all of them now. Is it alright with you? he asked.

– Just fire off, your words sound really interesting.

– It is clinging that I'm talking about. You cling to feelings as well, that is, you want to keep a feeling to yourself and not let it go. You'll do everything in your power not to let it go. This need to feel a certain feeling makes you avoid other feelings.

– Are you talking about pleasant feelings now?

– Both pleasant and unpleasant. The self doesn't care whether the feeling is pleasant or unpleasant, it is only interested in its own existence. Clinging is connected with hiding feelings. When you want to experience a certain feeling you always try to avoid another.

The man paused and gave me some time to think about what he had said. Perhaps this was so important that I really would have to find out what he meant.

– Hiding feelings may lead to addictions. In that case, the self needs an object and a certain feeling to hide the feeling it is avoiding. The object covers the feeling that is avoided, or at least numbs it temporarily. I mentioned earlier some of the different ways to do this. The self uses the need to help itself.

– What do you mean?

– The self makes you need something. It develops an addiction to some object and keeps itself alive with the help of this object.

– You are talking about the self as if it were a living creature that has to survive.

– The self needs something in order to survive. The self usually covers the unpleasant feeling either with a pleasant or a numbing feeling. A thought or some other object may temporarily cover the feeling in the background, and as I have already said, the self makes use of unpleasant feelings as well. It may cling to unpleasant feelings and even develop a role for itself with the help of the feelings. In that case, one identifies oneself with a thought, such as assuming the role of a victim or being ill. The roles of victim or patient provide the self with a chance to both suffer and survive at the same time. Then one identifies oneself with these unpleasant feelings and makes this condition a part of one's identity.

– I don't understand. If I feel I suffer, whatever the reason, then I suffer. I don't see how denying could be of any help, I said, getting a bit impatient.

– I'm not asking you to deny anything. I'm just asking you to look the feeling in the eye and leave it alone. If you don't cling to it, it will disappear sooner or later. The same goes for all the feelings you cover or deny. All feelings that produce suffering come and go if only you let them come and go.

– Well, but isn't that quite clear? Life is sometimes nice and sometimes it isn't.

– Who says so?

– Well, I do, and lots of others, I justified.

The man looked at me silently for a moment.

– When there is no self, there is no suffering, the man smiled gently.

Now it was my turn to be quiet.

– I don't suffer, he continued.

– Really? Never?

– There is no one anymore to cause me suffering.

– Well, here we go again. I just don't seem to grasp the meaning of your words. You too must feel something. Are you saying that you wouldn't feel anything if I hit you now?

– The body senses spontaneously through the five senses. One of the senses is feeling. The body might temporarily feel pain but there is no one any more in the body who would cause suffering. Suffering is caused by the self, while pain is a spontaneous reaction to a stimulus. As I told you earlier, all your feelings originate in your thoughts, if they are not spontaneous reactions to some stimuli. In this moment you can feel the breeze on your skin, your eyes see, your ears hear, your nose smells and your mouth tastes.

I calmed down for a moment to experience the world through all the senses.

– The most important thing is to observe where the suffering comes from. When there is nobody in you who causes imbalance with thoughts, there is no suffering either. You yourself never experience permanent balance because you yourself create the imbalance. The self will do anything in its power to find peace, which you already Have. There is no need to look for balance and peace; most important is to find the source that prevents you from experiencing balance and peace. People have innumerable symptoms, both physical and mental, and all these symptoms come from the self. Both physical and mental illnesses are becoming more and more common these days. If people knew what enslaves them, they would also realize where the source of all suffering lies: the self is the cause of all illnesses.

– That sounds a little distressing. As if I was responsible for my own suffering!

– As I already said, the self does anything to preserve its existence – it may even destroy the body to stay alive. I'm not telling you about the self so that you can feel guilty. I'm telling you about it so that you can get rid of all suffering. The real You is not an illusion that wants you to suffer. You Are something completely different.

– I don't really know what to think of all this, I said, shaking my head. – I have always thought that suffering is part of life. I have accepted the fact that I cannot simply be happy all the time.

– To your self happiness is something that comes and goes. The self tries to search for or keep something that you already Have. The self needs an object to be able to feel happy. This object brings happiness. If the self can't have an object of happiness, or if it loses it for some reason, happiness is no longer possible. Then the self suffers. The self makes use of the need to attain happiness.

Although it was difficult for me to understand the exact meaning of the man's words, something in them convinced me that they were not just full of hot air.

– One cannot gain or lose happiness. Happiness Is. Happiness doesn't need a special object. Suffering is caused by the fact that you yourself try to be happy.

– Do you mean that happiness isn't a feeling at all?

– The body feels. What you Are shines through the body. When there is nobody any more, everything that is left is what Is.

– That's not very easy to comprehend.

– I can't describe what you really Are because you would only form a thought of it you could identify with. I can help you only by telling you what you are not.

– And I'm not my feelings?

– Find out what is left when there is no yourself any more.

When there is no myself! I began to doubt whether I would ever be able to understand what the man was trying to say to me. How on earth could there be anything left if there was no myself? Then there would be no one to be aware of what is left! My thoughts were chaotic, tossing back and forth in my mind, and I didn't seem to be able to make head or tail of them.

– Feelings are a significant source of identification. If you let all the feelings just come and go I can promise you that you will realise what you really Are. You don't have to do anything. It's enough if you just leave everything alone.

I considered the man's words carefully. I even had a glimpse of something but couldn't hold onto it firmly.

– You mean, I just have to concentrate on the present moment? I muttered in the end.

– Exactly. Let the thoughts and feelings just come and go. Don't try to hide anything or cling to anything. You just have to follow everything unconditionally. What you Are, Is always in this moment.

– Sounds quite simple.

– Your self will do it's best not to just let everything Be. You need to trust Life. Without trust you dare not jump into the unknown.

– You're talking like I was setting off on a real adventure, I laughed timidly.

– You will sooner or later see the surprise I promised you. Just trust the Voice inside you, he answered, smiling.

I didn't say anything for the simple reason that I didn't know what to say. The man remained quiet too. I had a hunch that all of a sudden he didn't have anything more to say to me. Besides, it was getting late.

– I think I'll go to bed. I've got work tomorrow, I said stretching my sleepy limbs.

– Of course, the man nodded. – If you feel you'd like to talk later on you'll be quite sure to find me over there. He pointed at the little green tent a short distance away.

– Are you living in a tent? I asked curiously.

– No, I'm not living anywhere.

– So you're travelling all the time. You're on the road all the time? I asked, trying desperately to drag some information out of him.

– I'm not travelling anywhere, and I'm not on the road, or on anything, at that. I'm not here.

– Oh yes, I laughed shaking my head. – I guess it's high time to hit the hay.

The man didn't say anything.

– Thank you. It was nice talking to you again. I'll surely let you know when I've seen the surprise. I was a little amused. The man said he wasn't here but could be found in the tent anyway. I didn't understand at the time that I saw the man here because I was here myself. For the same reason the man talked to me here although He wasn't here Himself any more. The body was only an instrument for Him to use here, nothing else.

– All right, the man laughed warmly. Good night.

– Yeah, a real good night.

9

You are not your identity

During the next few days I watched myself like a hawk. After the evening I spent with the man I realized for the first time what a mess my mind really was. I had never before been aware of the fact that my thoughts were bouncing here and there all the time. The meditation practice had particularly opened my eyes. I didn't understand what the man had tried to explain – his thoughts just seemed interesting to me. I was still very sure that I was Sanna, and it was only curiosity that led me to observe my thoughts. I was also very eager to tell Jani everything the man had said but my new acquaintance didn't seem to interest him very much. He thought that the man's stories sounded strange, to say the least. I understood Jani very well since I didn't understand myself what the man had tried to explain.

I tried to concentrate on the present moment as well as I could. I drank my coffee in the morning in small sips without gulping it down in a hurry. At work I tried to concentrate only on thinning the apples from the trees. I listened to the birds singing, and dropped small fruits to the ground. I noticed soon, however, that the more I tried to concentrate on what I was doing in the moment, the more easily my thoughts seemed to flee elsewhere. (My thoughts were fleeing elsewhere all the time, of course, but I wasn't always aware of that.)

After a few days I became impatient. I had really seen no surprise. My own thoughts began to disturb me. The working days seemed long. It was always so quiet on the farm: only Jani and me thinning out the apple trees. In the middle of this silence my own thoughts started to echo in my head. Gradually, I got the feeling that something was bothering me. I was tired of listening to myself. Of course this thought seemed really amusing to me. How could I be bothering myself?

All kinds of thoughts were rolling through my mind. The future plans still occupied my mind most of the time. I felt restless because I didn't know what we were going to do after getting back to Finland. Christmas was coming, so my thoughts were moving constantly to my closest ones and life in Finland. As well as the future, my thoughts seemed to also move into the past. I noticed that all kinds of memories were surging into my consciousness. I thought of my childhood and life in general. I was going through my own story. My mind was flooded with all kinds of memories from over the years, some of which I hadn't thought about for a long time. My feelings changed from one moment to another. I laughed by myself, then the next moment I could feel the tears running down my cheeks. I tried to follow my thoughts objectively, as the man had suggested. Little by little, my attention was especially drawn to my body and the sensations the thoughts created within it. I clearly noticed that certain type of thoughts caused a certain type of reaction. A certain thought could really be felt in my body in a certain way. A certain meaning aroused a certain feeling. This observation was stunning. After all, it was me, myself, that was the source of my feelings.

I decided to go and meet the man. There was something fascinating in him, something very interesting. I knew instinctively that he might really know something about life. Never before had I talked about life so deeply, not even with Jani. I had always just lived without giving it any contemplative thought. Now my interest was aroused for some reason. I noticed that I had a burning desire to know everything the man knew. The whole situation seemed really funny to me. I soon went to the small, green tent.

– Huh-hoo, the unconceivable, are you there? I didn't know by what other name I could have called him.

– Oh, hello. Nice to see you, the man said pushing his head out of the tent.

– Have you got a minute?

– Sure.

The man crawled out of the tent, and we both sat down on the grass.

– I've done what you suggested and followed my thoughts and the feelings reflected in them.

– And?

– Interesting, really interesting, I said with wrinkled brow.

– There's something in this that confuses me. Could you explain a bit more exactly what you mean by the self? Last time you asked me to find out what's left when there is no myself any more. You talked as if the self is something that's separate from me. What do you actually mean by this?

– We really have to dig in deeper to this now. As I mentioned before, your idea of what you are – I mean what you think you are – and at the same time your idea of the truth comes from your identification with your body. Who or what were you before you got your name?

– A baby, I said knowingly.

– All right, a baby is a good example because it is unqualified. Let's use that. As a baby you weren't Sanna yet. You had no idea of who you were. You began to build the concept of yourself only later. Nothing was personal to you when you were a baby. You reacted to stimuli spontaneously, you probably cried when you were hungry but you didn't think: "Oh, now I'm hungry!" Crying was a spontaneous reaction, not a personal experience.

– You're wrong now. We are influenced by all our experiences. The first years, especially, are very important. How the baby is treated will affect the rest of its life. Already the first months are very important to the tiny, new creature.

– Affect whom? he asked calmly.

– To the baby, naturally, or the person that the baby will be when it grows up.

– Right. So there has to be someone who can be influenced by experiences.

– Naturally. Without the baby there is no one who could experience.

– Does the baby need itself to react spontaneously? Or does one need oneself in general to react spontaneously? Do you need yourself right now to be able to sit here with me? Do you need yourself to have the breeze touching your face?

– In my opinion, I can't do anything without myself.

– I understand. But let's go back to the baby, or actually the time when you became aware of yourself. This awareness of yourself started when you identified yourself with your body and with everything that the body brings into your consciousness through the five senses. Little by little the creation of the self started, the self that gave and still gives everything that happens to you a meaning using the body as an instrument. The self started to take advantage of the body in which it found a splendid means to exist. The moment you identified yourself with your body, you were born. The body and the self walk hand in hand.

– I think I was born when I came out of my mother's womb!

– Your body was born then, but you yourself were born when you became aware of yourself.

– I don't understand.

– Your life began when you began to form meanings. Your parents and the rest of your environment helped you at the start. Your self got a name, which in your case is Sanna. When you learned your name the conception of your self got a firm basis. On this basis the self started to develop and gain strength. Briefly, you started to do your best to keep yourself, the illusion, alive. By identifying with your body, Sanna got a home for her developing identity. When you learned to talk, you were able to orally express the meanings you had given the forms. The more meanings you formed, the more personal everything became. You couldn't think if you hadn't formed meanings. Each thought has a meaning of its own. These meanings were born when you learned to give names to things in your environment. You have yourself developed the reality you believe in. Everything you see has a meaning for you.

– I'm not sure I can follow you now.

– With the help of meanings, your identity and simultaneously your environment, your life, started to get a shape. You don't see life as it Is. You see life through the meanings you have formed yourself. You have developed your life using these meanings. All your experiences have been formed from these meanings. You can't create memories without meanings. All memories are just thoughts. All your life is composed of mere thoughts.

I looked at him wondering what this was all about.

– What's that? he asked pointing to a tree near us.

– A tree, I answered, without a moment's hesitation.

– How do you know it's a tree?

– Because it is a tree, I answered with a happy laugh.

– Be a little more exact.

– Because it looks like a tree, I said astonished and amused. – It has a stem and leaves like trees.

– Well, have you seen many trees during your life?

I decided to join in the fun.

– Quite a few, I guess. Here in Manjimup the trees are a bit like trees in Finland, only a little bigger. There was a rainforest near Cairns and there were small twisted stumps in the Outback.

– So you have an entire tree collection of memories in your mind? he asked smiling broadly.

– Yeah, I guess so.

– When you were small and saw your first tree you didn't know what it was. You looked at it without a meaning. As you notice now you have several meanings for a tree at present. You don't see the tree as it Is, you only see the tree as an idea, a memory.

– Oh. What Is a tree then? I looked at the tree, still amused.

– The need to make it something is the same as giving it a meaning. To be able to see everything as it Is, you have to let every meaning you have formed just be.

– Are you saying that I don't see right?

– You see everything through the meanings of your own. To be able to shake off all the meanings from your shoulders you will have to let every thought, every meaning, come and go. The meanings are not a problem. It's enough to simply perceive how your mind works.

I stared at the tree quietly trying to see it without the meaning I had given it.

– Your whole identity was formed in the same way as the tree. You have used meanings to create experiences and these experiences form your story. You have made up – and are constantly making up – your own story. You're carrying a sack on your back that is full of memories, thoughts about yourself. The whole story called Sanna is only a bunch of thoughts. Nothing else.

– I guess you are talking about my self now, I said confused.

– Yes, I'm talking about your shell, the I, the illusion you believe in.

– I must say this sounds interesting. I do know I'm Sanna and you are claiming quite seriously that she is only an illusion!

– Your reality is hanging from a thread and that thread can be very thick, but it's still only a thread.

I glanced at the tree again and wasn't at all sure of what I should see and think.

10

The illusion of separateness

– You consider yourself a separate individual, an individual who has thoughts. You believe you were born when you came out of your mother's womb and that you will die when your body stops functioning. You believe you are a body, a thinking body.

– Y-e-es, maybe you can put it that way too, I mumbled.

– This illusion according to which you are a thinking body provides the root for all other illusions you believe in as well. One of these other illusions is a thought that you are something that is separate from others. The moment you began to identify yourself with your body you began to feel you're separate. You began to believe that you are something that is separate from all others. You began to develop your own identity and observe your environment as separate objects. To you everything existed, and is still existing, as pieces. The feeling of separateness is true to you because otherwise you wouldn't even exist.

– Yes, I am I, and you are you. And then there's this tree and everything else, I admitted.

– The feeling of separateness is part of the illusion. What you really Are is not separate from anything, it is everywhere and in everything. It has always been and will always be. You are everything that Is.

– Sounds pretty wild and rather unreal. I don't feel I'm everywhere and in everything, I said.

– Of course not. You identify yourself with your self.

I remained quiet.

– And because you identify yourself with your self and at the same time with your body, you believe that you were born and that you will die. Because the body is not permanent you feel you're not permanent either. This is part of the illusion according to which you exist as a self. It's a big illusion because what you Are in reality was never born and will never die – it just Is.

– A-all right, I said curtly because I didn't know what else to say. Nobody had ever said anything like this to me before.

– Let's go back to this feeling of separateness. It is so comprehensive that it provides a basis for all your actions. You might not consider this feeling peculiar at all because it is your normal condition. This doesn't mean, however, that it is your natural condition, simply that you're used to it. The feeling of separateness is preserved with the help of comparing: you compare everything all the time.

– What do you mean?

– You compare everything to be able to form meanings. Something can't exist without something else, and without something else you couldn't exist yourself.

– Well, I guess I lost the plot again.

– Comparing is normal to you. You've been used to it since you were a small child. You form a picture of yourself by comparison. Comparing you know who you are.

– Could you explain that a little more clearly?

– The whole idea of yourself has been formed by comparison. You have created your whole identity by reflecting yourself to your environment. You began by reflecting yourself first to your parents and your siblings if you had them, and later when your environment grew larger, you went on comparing yourself to other people. And now I'm not only talking about every person you have met during your lifetime but also of everything you have interiorized in the interaction with your environment. You are full of ideas about yourself and each image is only an illusion.

– Well, it is true that children imitate their parents, I pondered aloud.

– As a child you interiorized all the behaviour patterns, principles and ideals of your parents and formed the concept of yourself according to the feedback you got from them. As your living environment grew larger, the feedback became larger. By comparing yourself with your environment you shaped – and are still shaping – your identity, your idea of yourself. Your environment plays an important role in the formation of your identity. Society, the media and the era you're living in all have a strong effect on you. The norms and ideals of the society sometimes create objectives that are not uttered aloud. I'm sure you have an idea of what you should be like. As to that, the media takes care of a big part of it, and today it is one of the mightiest influences in life. You believe in your environment and by believing in it you create a picture of yourself.

– I do understand that when I was a child I believed everything my parents said to me, but nowadays I think with my own brain. It's not the media or society either that makes my decisions.

– That's right. At first you interiorized everything without asking questions, but as you gained more experience you began to form your own opinions, your own conceptions of the truth. You began to believe yourself instead of your environment. But your own opinions too are based on comparison: you either compare an opinion of yours with the opinion of the environment or you compare it with an opinion you yourself had before. Opinions are meanings and all meanings have been formed by yourself. All you form yourself is based on believing; yourself wouldn't exist without believing.

– I guess you will have to be a bit more exact again.

– Your idea of yourself is based on believing. Since you believe that you yourself and your environment are two separate things, you either believe your environment or yourself. Do you understand?

– I think so. My opinions are not necessarily compatible with those of the environment.

– Your reality – and at the same time your identity – has been constructed from different meanings, which you have formed yourself by practising comparison. After that both your opinions and your experiences are born with the help of meanings. Your whole identity is held together by separate meanings. You believe you are a separate individual, a person who has their own thoughts; you believe you are a story composed of memories.

– Oh yes, I do have opinions of all kinds, and quite a lot of memories too, I mumbled more to myself than to the man.

– You can't let your self – the sack of memories – drop from your shoulders until you stop comparing.

– But why should I want to forget my memories? It seems to me you are hinting that my memories are an awful burden to me.

– You don't have to forget anything. It is enough for you to take the sack from your shoulders, put it down and leave it alone. You are not that sack.

I looked at the man in confusion. I didn't really get what he meant.

– It doesn't matter whether the sack is full of good or bad memories. You can't fly until you put your sack down, the man said with a warm smile I knew only too well now.

– And I can't put the sack down as long as I compare?

– No, you can't.

I realized all of a sudden that I really was comparing everything all the time, not only myself with all the others, but everything around me. All my opinions and memories were formed by comparing them with something else. I began to feel a bit restless.

– Are you saying that comparing is wrong?

– No, it isn't wrong, but it maintains the illusion. The feeling of separateness is preserved as long as there is somebody who compares.

– Well then, is the feeling of separateness wrong?

– No, there's nothing wrong in that either – it is only an illusion.

– So there is nothing wrong in my feeling of being a separate individual?

– No, there isn't. There's nothing wrong in anything. It is only an illusion.

– Well, what harm does an illusion do then?

– There's no harm in the illusion. It just simply isn't true.

Once again I didn't know what to think. Sometimes I felt that the man was just playing with words, and perhaps with my thoughts as well, and that his only purpose was to confuse me.

– Nevertheless, let's concentrate on comparing for another moment, and on the feeling of separateness it creates, if it's alright with you, the man suggested with his delightfully easy-going way.

– Yes, it's all right with me, I said a little absent-mindedly because all kinds of thoughts were whirling in my head.

– I'm sure you recognize comparing in yourself, otherwise you wouldn't have asked me if comparing was wrong. Is that so?

– Yes, it is. I have to admit that I compare everything continuously, I nodded humbly.

– That's a good observation as it makes you notice how the self preserves its existence. Without the self there would be no comparing for without it there would be nothing to compare anymore. Comparing can be clearly seen all over the world. Everyone learns sooner or later that life is a competition, a game that each individual plays alone. You are competing with yourself and with your environment, and you will always find an object you can compare yourself or something else to. By comparing you feel either more or less than, either better or worse than something else, depending on the object you're comparing yourself with. The competition that arises from constant comparing is endless, and will always lead to the eternal feeling of insufficiency.

– That is perfectly true. Nowadays life is merely performing and achieving. Nothing is ever enough, I said with a sigh.

– Nothing will ever be enough permanently, not for you or for your environment – it is completely impossible. The self will never feel permanently satisfied. The self will never be permanently enough – not for itself or for others. The self feels constant lack. Some object may temporarily hide the feeling of lack, but as soon as the object that has hidden it is lost or cannot be attained, the self feels this insidious feeling again. I use the word insidious when I'm talking about the lack and feeling of insufficiency, for it is a feeling that is always affecting you in the background, even though the person themselves don't wish to admit it.

– Are you trying to hint something? I asked, smiling timidly.

– Perhaps, he said benevolently.

– It is quite true that I'm never permanently satisfied. Maybe it's caused by that very feeling of insufficiency.

– The feeling of insufficiency is based on the feeling of separateness. That takes us back to one of the most significant illusions created by the self: separateness. All your actions are guided by the feeling of being separate. This feeling of separateness leads to the bottomless yearning, the yearning to belong to something, the yearning to be part of something. You feel that you are missing something. You feel you are alone, and this feeling of loneliness makes you long for this something. You don't want to be alone. You are afraid of being alone.

It is true that I was afraid of being alone earlier. I just hadn't thought what the reason for this might be. It is a double bind: we feel we are alone and we are afraid of being alone, so instead of trying to find out what it is in the loneliness that scares us, we fabricate all kinds of means, excuses and explanations to be able to imagine that we are not alone after all. We run away from our loneliness instead of looking at it eye to eye.

– But you are not alone. The feeling of loneliness only comes from the feeling of separateness. And both of these feelings are born when you identify yourself with your self, in other words, you believe in the illusion. These feelings are true to you as long as you don't know what you really Are. When you know what you really Are you won't feel lonely any more – it will be impossible. You won't be then alone rather You Are One. Because you don't know what you really Are, you are afraid – your little self is afraid – to be alone; you are actually afraid of what you really Are.

– I'm afraid of what I really Am! I don't get it.

– You do everything in your power to make the disgusting feeling in the background disappear. You cover the feeling using different means, you even deny it is there. The man looked deep into my eyes.

I felt nervous and I didn't even know why. The man kept smiling at me gently and soothingly.

– You try to cover the feeling of loneliness – and at the same time the feeling of separateness – by seeking groups of people you feel you belong to. The most important group is usually your family and other relations close to you. It may also be your nationality, religion, ideology, team or even a brand of clothing. Any group is good enough as long as you feel you belong. There is the we-phenomenon at the back of that. Along with that you feel you are part of others, a part of the group called we.

– Yes, absolutely right. I don't want to be alone. I need others near me.

– I don't mean that you should strive to be alone. I only want you to notice how the self preserves its existence.

At this point I didn't yet realize the fact that I didn't have to do anything to anything; it was enough just to observe how things are.

– Identifying yourself with a group can never hide the feeling of lack – it cannot give you a permanent feeling of togetherness, for it was the comparing in the first place that made you look for a particular group to belong to. And you remember that comparing comes from the feeling of separateness. It is an endless circle that feeds itself. There would be no groups at all if there was no feeling of separateness, and along with it the need to belong to something.

– And what are you really aiming at with all these explanations?

– I'm trying to help you understand that you don't really know what you really Are. All groups and all classifications on the whole are the result of the fact that people do not know their true Being.

– Well, it would be really nice if we could all live in peace together. But the world just isn't like that.

– Remember that the environment is only a reflection of yourself. You can't find an answer somewhere out there, you'll find it in yourself.

I didn't say anything. I suddenly felt very sad. A feeling of guilt was peeping from behind my shoulder. I didn't understand at the time that the man did by no means want me to feel guilty about anything. He just wanted to make me realize something very important.

– By separating, the self breaks the whole into pieces. By comparing it classifies everything into parts. Because the whole appears to you as separate objects, the self is able to preserve its own existence. Without something else, the self would naturally be nothing.

You try to cover the feeling of separateness created by these scattered pieces by belonging to different groups. You want to be part of something. You miss what you Are.

The man paused and looked at me.

– Your need to belong to something may also have roots in the fear of being different. You may oppose or even be afraid of everything that's different. Being different may even disgust or irritate you. It may feel disgusting because you don't really want to be different, separate. All discrimination and racism is connected with the very fear of being different. The fear of being different causes many people to identify themselves with the mainstream or some common cause. Belonging to a group brings safety. You are like a dog chasing its own tail.

– Do you mean that I'm trying to be separate myself but at the same time I'd like to be whole?

– Yes. This is the conflict you are living in.

– Mmm... interesting.

I had always wondered why people considered each other unequal. Now I had got at least one possible answer. I didn't actually yet understand what there was behind all this but I had premonitions. At the level of thought the man's words started to sound more and more interesting.

– You cover the feeling of separateness by owning as well. By owning something you feel you belong. By possessing you become part of the object you possess: you are part of something and something is part of you. In this way, you identify yourself with the thought "mine". The mine-thought is often connected with a group, in which case the mine-thought becomes an our-thought. By possessing you try to hide the feeling of lack. You want to possess more and more and cling tooth and nail to what you feel you already own. You want for yourself – that is, for me – and for everyone belonging to you –that is, to us – and then you think you want for others too. You work on your identity with the objects you possess. By possessing you preserve the existence of your self.

The man gave me a moment to let his words sink in.

– How do you mean I think I want for others too? I genuinely want the best for those near me.

– You see everyone near you as a separate creature from you, but in fact they are all part of you. You don't even notice how you identify yourself with the people who are important to you, so you imagine that you could unselfishly want something for them. However in reality you only want for yourself, because you have unconditionally identified yourself with the persons close to you.

This was something I could not digest just like that: It can't be true that I only have selfish aspirations even when I really want something good for somebody else.

– No, that just can't be true. I really want something good for others too.

– Yes, but you just don't understand that all the objects you own – including the people you consider important to you – are part of yourself: you feel you are what you own. If you lose the object you own, the feeling of lack you try to hide rises to the surface again. When you feel you've lost something you immediately need something else in its place. You might even feel desperate. You try to cover this feeling of lack by possessing more and more. You don't understand that nothing outside you will ever be enough. By possessing you try to fill the bottomless well.

– I admit that nowadays people buy lots of things. The western countries, particularly, suffer from consumption hysteria.

– Still, I'm not only talking about the material things. You feel you are part of everything you think you possess. Any thought is enough as long as the object is your own. Many people regard their nationality, religion, ideology, skill, family and even the planet earth as their own. The more tightly you identify yourself with an object that you think you own, the tighter you cling to it. You need the object. You are part of that object. You may even feel that you can't live without the object.

The man paused briefly and looked with exploration into my eyes.

– You even think you own your own life. What would you be if you had no self?

I felt something was breaking inside me. The man's words had obviously touched a sore point.

– But I do exist, I stammered. – I don't understand at all what you mean.

– Don't worry, I can see what situation you're in, but as I've already said, you try to cover the feeling of lack by possessing. You'll do whatever it takes not to face the feeling of lack. You don't understand that by bravely facing that feeling you could wake up to realize what you really Are.

– Do you mean that I should get rid of everything I own?

– No. Nothing external can change what you Are. By changing your life you can in no way change what you really Are. It is enough if you just observe how the self preserves its existence.

– That's exactly what is so difficult for me to grasp.

– You don't have to do or change anything – you are already enough. You just believe you aren't enough. You believe that something's got to change. This takes us again back to the feeling of insufficiency and separateness, in other words to your self.

– Do you mean that I am already perfect? I wondered aloud.

– Yes. You are perfect. You just don't know you are perfect because you don't know who you really Are.

This thought seemed very alien to me. I didn't feel perfect at all.

– So, I seek my way into some groups and feel the need to possess because I don't feel I'm enough?

– Yes. The need comes from the feeling of lack. As long as you don't know what you really Are you need something, in other words, you feel lack.

– But you have to eat, too, for example.

– The body needs nourishment to keep alive. What I Am and what you Are too doesn't want or need anything. It just gives. And because It just gives, It also receives for there is nothing else that exists but It's Self.

– I think I'm going to scream because I don't seem to understand what you are trying to say.

– There's no need to worry, you'll understand in the long run. Let's go back to the illusion of separateness. You don't want to give anything if you don't get anything in return because if you just give you feel you have to part with something. And when you give up something the feeling of lack rises to the surface. You can only give when you believe you will get something in return.

This could in no way be contradicted: the man was perfectly right.

– There is no one else. That is what you don't want to understand yourself. That is what the self doesn't want you to understand.

I sighed deeply again – who knows how many times I had already done that. My head was like a carousel; not one thought seemed to stay in its own place, all my thoughts were going round and round in circles. The man must have noticed my dilemma because he seemed to become serious all of a sudden.

– I think it's time you got some rest. We've had a long conversation.

– I agree, I said with a faint smile.

– Remember what I said: just leave everything be, let each thought just come and go. Observe yourself without prejudice. Observe what it is in you that compares and wants to belong. Observe what it is in you that discriminates and doesn't want to be alone. Observe what it is in you that feels itself separate and insufficient, what in you feels the need to possess and join groups.

– That's quite a lot to think about, I said rubbing my forehead.

– That's quite understandable and there's nothing wrong with it. You are allowed to think, he said smiling his irresistible smile.

I got up stiffly.

– Thank you, it was really interesting to talk to you. Maybe I'll soon see the surprise you promised.

– I'm sure you will – sooner or later.

– See you.

– Yeah, it seems like it.

PART TWO

The shell cracks

11

The illusion of guilt

During the next few days I continued to observe my thoughts. I noticed I was still thinking a lot about the future as well as the past. Thoughts just popped up into my mind one after another. I tried to observe myself objectively but it became more and more difficult as the days went by. The continuous chatter in my head began to disturb me more and more. I got frustrated because I couldn't concentrate on the present moment. I kept shaking my head wondering why I hadn't paid any attention to my thoughts before. The thoughts really disturbed me, and the distraction increased when I noticed they were getting darker and gloomier day by day.

At first, I tried to push all the unpleasant thoughts away. I talked with Jani or counted how many small apples I had already dropped on the ground. But the annoying thoughts were stubborn. The worry particularly started to knock at my door. First it came in the shape of my own future, but soon it changed form, commenting on what might have happened to my family and friends. Next it brought famine and climate change with it. I noticed I was turning over the problems of the planet in my mind – and by no means was this the first time. I had been a worrier all my life. However this time the worries really began to swell right in front of my eyes. I kept sighing deeply, trying to find solutions to all the world's problems.

The higher the pile of problems I stacked in my mind, the more guilt followed. Memories from Kenya, in particular, kept surging in my mind. I had done my practical training in Africa seven years earlier. I had spent three months in an environment that was completely different to anywhere I'd lived until then. The slums, street kids and overall poverty made a huge impression on me. I spent most of my time in the countryside near a small village called Tonay. A couple of other Finns and I slept in a house that had been reserved for us, whereas our neighbours lived in clay huts a couple of meters away. During this time, I had the opportunity to get acquainted with local traditions and living conditions. After returning to Finland, I saw my own life in a different light. I had wanted to do my practical training abroad because I had felt the need to get away from Finland. I wanted to experience something new and completely different. After returning to Finland, I was grateful for everything. I felt I was lucky to have been born in Finland. Having clean water just by turning on the tap felt like a real miracle. I stopped complaining about petty matters, and decided to enjoy life.

With the gratefulness came the guilt. Guilt was like a shadow that followed me everywhere. I felt guilty because I wanted to enjoy life instead of helping people in Africa. Helping them would have meant moving there and living in the middle of the clay huts. But I wanted to live in Finland near my loved ones, I wanted to travel and be happy. Naturally the guilt appeared in various other forms too. Every so often it found a good reason to exist. The clearest form it took when it appeared to me, was in the thought of saving others. (I had had guilty feelings all my life. Guilt is one of the most powerful and significant means by which the self preserves its existence.)

By observing my thoughts I saw my guilt clearly. I had a bad conscience and I started to feel worse. I pondered whether I was doing the right thing in making my dream come true. I was also worried about what would happen if I didn't live my life in the right way. For the first time I started to contemplate death, and didn't know what to think of it. I was still strongly convinced I was Sanna who will die when breathing stops. I began to think of the possibility of life going on after death. The man's ideas of eternal life had clearly made a strong impression on me. For the first time in my life, death began to frighten me. What if I'll be thrown into some kind of hell because I hadn't behaved properly? I had always been a good girl and a fine citizen, a so-called good person. What if all that wasn't enough? I even asked Jani what he thought. Jani looked at me a bit worried and asked if I was all right. In his opinion, there was no point thinking about death. I had been of the same opinion before but now my thoughts had changed. For some reason or other, I became interested in what death really meant. The conversations with the man had set me thinking. (In fact, I wasn't thinking about death for the first time, but in Manjimup I began to ponder this subject consciously).

Nearly a week went by before I had the next conversation with the man. I had a day off and decided to go and see whether the man was alone near his tent. I had seen him a couple of times but he had always been in company. I felt I needed a private conversation with him.

The man was contentedly drinking tea when I appeared in front of him with my questions.

– Hi.

– Well, hello, the man said, smiling happily.

– How are you? I asked in a forced way, trying to be polite.

– Fine, if there was somebody who could be fine, he answered with a laugh. – And you?

– I've kept on observing my thoughts, I answered seriously.

– And?

– Interesting, still very interesting. I can't believe I've never paid attention to what a lot of thoughts are constantly crossing my mind. Something is going on there all the time. There's no way I could concentrate only on the present moment. It's quite impossible because my thoughts are always somewhere else. The endless chatter in my head just goes on and on.

– Let the thoughts just roll on. There's nothing wrong with thoughts. It is enough that you just observe them. Be like a spectator in the front row at the theatre.

– But I'm not able to do that. I have to think of certain things.

– Well, allow thinking and watch the thinker. Let the actor perform his role and watch the performance.

The idea that I wouldn't be the one who is thinking, in other words acting a role in a performance called life, but that I would be "somebody" just watching this thinker and the performance, is by no means new, but this was the first time in my life I had heard about it. For some reason the idea didn't seem strange to me at all, but weirdly quite familiar and natural. I didn't understand then why I felt what I felt. Now it's crystal clear to me: the strange premonition was my Friend, a Friend Who was knocking at the door of my consciousness.

– I'm sure that lots of things are rising into your consciousness, things that you've never thought or didn't want to think of before.

I nodded and sat down beside him.

– Is some particular thing bothering you?

– Quite a few things, but particularly... I couldn't finish my sentence. My voice began to tremble and tears ran down my cheeks. The man hugged me gently, and didn't say anything. I was surprised by my reaction.

– I am scared I'm not living right, I stammered.

– There's no way you could live wrong. It's just impossible.

– But there's so much evil in life. I don't understand why people behave the way they do. I don't understand why I behave the way I do. This planet is sick. I'm very sick myself.

– Why do you think so? The man asked calmly.

– I allow innocent children to die. I'm not doing anything although I've seen with my own eyes how people are suffering. I'm just enjoying life. Don't you think that's sick?

– You feel guilty, the man said, as if he was stating an indisputable fact.

– I've been pondering life on this planet. Everything is sick somehow. I just don't get it. I don't understand myself. Why do people want to fight wars and quarrel with each other? Why am I not helping children?

– Why do you want to help children?

I glared at the man, his words taking me by surprise.

– Because they are suffering.

– You want to eliminate suffering because you are suffering yourself. It is you who doesn't want to suffer any more.

I was sobbing for a while because I really did have a guilty conscience.

– That's true. I don't want to suffer and I don't want anyone else to suffer either.

– This is a big step. Now you only have to find out what or who causes your suffering.

– That's exactly what's so terrible in all this. How can anyone on this planet stop suffering? I don't understand life. There's no sense in it. There's no sense in anything, not even in this. I'm living my dream and bawling here now when I'm with you. There's no sense in that either!

Suddenly it dawned on me how foolish even my complaints sounded.

– You are observing yourself at the moment. You are trying to understand why the self acts as it acts. But there's no sense in the actions of the self, it only wants to preserve its existence. Nothing else.

– I'm talking about life now. All this. There's no sense in all life, I said, pointing at everything around us.

– I know what you mean. To be able to understand life you have to understand yourself.

– What do you mean? I don't understand anything about anything, I sighed deeply.

– Let's talk about this fear you've invented for yourself, the fear of not living right. Is that alright with you?

I nodded reluctantly.

– Guilt is one of the most powerful ways the self uses to survive. You feel guilty because you make yourself feel guilty – you judge yourself. For the same reason you make others feel guilty. On the basis of your experiences, you have formed opinions, ideas of right and wrong, and on the basis of these ideas you have developed rules and behaviour patterns for yourself. You act according to them. You are playing a game you have made up yourself, a game whose rules you have chosen yourself.

I was dumbfounded.

– Do you think life is just a game?

– I'm talking about you yourself now. You have developed thoughts which you have classified either right or wrong, according to your own taste. You have made up a game that suits you, and you are playing that game with yourself right now. You may try to play the game right or not, but it doesn't make any difference in the end as it is just a game you have made up.

– What game are you talking about?

– There is no right or wrong. It is just you yourself who wants to classify thoughts according to your own conceptions.

– I'm not sure I get that. You can't do whatever you like.

– Who says so?

– Well, me and many others. I mean, there's got to be rules in life.

– Who says so?

I remained quiet. I didn't know what to say. To me it was perfectly clear that there had to be rules.

– You're playing a game, a game you have made up yourself, the man continued.

I began to get nervous. The idea of life as a mere game frightened me.

– Do you mean that killing isn't wrong?

– I don't mean anything. I'm just encouraging you to consider who decides the rules of the game.

I was completely astonished.

– You're moving your piece on the board on the basis of your own opinions; in other words, of your thoughts that are based on your experiences. Your every decision is based on what you think is right or wrong.

– If somebody came now and shot you, wouldn't you think that's wrong?

– Why would anyone come and shoot me?

– Well, I don't know. This planet is full of all kinds of lunatics.

– The self is only able to attack or defend. It does everything it can to preserve its existence.

– What!? You didn't answer my question.

– The answer is right in front of your nose, but because you want to hear something else, you don't hear the answer. You have to dig deeper than where you can get by judging. By judging you make up the rules of your game and you move your piece on the board according to those rules. Judging enables blame, and blame leads to condemnation. The self needs guilt to be able to survive. The self has to invent different kinds of rules and action patterns to be able to survive. The self doesn't want you to be Free, it wants you to feel guilty.

I didn't say anything, but looked at the man suspiciously.

– Nobody is judging you but yourself, he continued dispassionately.

– You're talking about the self again as if it was something separate from me. I really don't get it.

– You are not the self that wants you to feel guilty. Without identifying yourself with the maker of the game you couldn't even feel guilty. You would understand that there is no game. When there's nobody to feel guilty and make others feel guilty, there's nobody who decides in what direction to move the piece on the board. Then there's nobody who plays.

– So there's nobody judging me? Isn't there a god who judges my life? Can I do whatever I want? I asked the questions more to myself than the man.

– There's only you yourself that judges, nobody else. You yourself have developed the idea of a god that judges. The self is very cunning: it makes you play a game which you should win. It keeps up the illusion that there is something to win. It holds the imaginary prize right in front of your nose but doesn't actually ever want you to get it. The self doesn't want you to know that there is no victory or prize after all. It just wants you to continue the game, the game that you think you could win some day.

I gaped at the man with my mouth open.

– I urge you to observe what part in you feels the need to criticize, accuse and judge. It is this part of you that wants you to play the game, the game you have made up yourself.

– So you believe that I can never do anything wrong, I said, interrupting him.

– No one can ever do anything wrong – and I don't believe, I know. And you can know too if you just stop playing the game.

– Do you mean that, for example, Pol Pot didn't do anything wrong?

When I was in Cambodia I had visited a place called The Fields of Death. It was one of the areas where the consequences of Pol Pot's tyrannical regime could clearly be seen. Approximately twenty-five per cent of Cambodia's population was killed and many people were tortured because of the thoughts that Pol Pot and his followers considered right. The cruelty of human beings made me feel sick.

– Pol Pot was living in a dream, he was in a really deep sleep. He listened to himself. The self does everything in its power to preserve its existence.

The serenity and calmness with which he uttered those words made me gasp.

– Are you at all acquainted with the history of Cambodia? It is inconceivably cruel.

– The self does anything to preserve its existence, he repeated calmly.

– What on earth do you mean by the self? You talk as if it was a sick monster that is the source of all evil.

– You can describe it however you like. You're just playing a game.

– How come I'm just playing a game?

– There is nothing that's right or wrong in the self. The self is not a sin or an ideal. It just is what it is. The self just wants to survive. You can't understand what I'm saying until you are able to step aside and watch the game neutrally as an outsider.

– Does this mean that I have to accept everything?

– You have to see everything as it is – without prejudice, judgments, accusations and condemnation.

The man paused briefly again, allowing me some time to understand his words.

– You are looking at Life through a dusty window. You don't see Life, you just see the dust.

– What on earth does that mean in practice? I exclaimed indignantly, because the man's eternal symbols were beginning to get on my nerves.

– Just let all the thoughts come and go freely. Step aside and watch the game, don't take part in it. Observe the game without judging, accusing and condemning.

– That sounds really weird – nearly insane!

– Observing neutrally is difficult for you because you have made up the game yourself. You yourself desire to play it.

Gradually my indignation settled down and I was able to think more clearly.

– Don't you ever feel guilty, I asked him.

– Never. Nothing is personal to me any more. The game continues as long as there is somebody who plays it.

– Interesting, really interesting, I sighed.

The man smiled at me warmly and took a sip of tea. Soon he stood up.

– The tea is cold. I'll go and make some more. Do you want some?

– Oh, no! I've spoilt your tea, I exclaimed with a start. The maker of the game didn't really want to stop playing.

– You didn't spoil anything. I like talking to you.

I looked at the man for a while and tried to make up my mind as to what to do. I didn't want to disturb him but I didn't want to end the conversation either. I decided to trust the man and what he said.

– A nice cup of tea would be fine, I smiled happily.

We both went to the kitchen area of the camping ground and brewed some more tea. The man seemed to be in a good mood and very relaxed. I felt a certain lightness when I was with him. He didn't do anything special, he was just available to me. Later on, I understood that he wasn't just available but it was in fact that he actually wasn't there that made ”his” Presence so easy.

12

Free will

We carried our tea cups out of the kitchen area and sat down on the benches nearby. It was peaceful in the camping area. There were gusts of wind in the air and it would probably rain soon.

– You will find more fears that imprison you, the man said. – Fears are real to you because you create them yourself. You need courage to be able to look at your fears eye to eye. The self does everything possible in order not to die. It is a master of creating fears; it is a fear in itself.

– What do you mean, a fear in itself? I exclaimed to the man with furrowed brow.

– The self prevents you from listening to the inner Voice. It invents different kinds of fears in order to keep you prisoner. When you listen to your fears you follow your self.

– Really?

– Your every decision is based either on Love or fear. Love frees you, fear imprisons you.

– I do believe in love but I still can't deny the fact that there are many dangers in life. It's a good thing to feel scared sometimes, I said, trying to come up with a sensible excuse for being afraid.

– Why?

– When I'm scared I don't thrust my hand into a fire or walk onto the road with my eyes shut, for instance. Fear prevents me from
hurting myself.

– You don't need fear to keep yourself safe. You can use your memories without fear. You can react spontaneously and avoid the danger
without any fear. Danger, of course, is something that threatens your
body but because you're not your body there can be no real danger.
It is also important for you to notice that most of your fears have
nothing to do with spontaneous occasions which always occur in
the present moment. Fear is usually connected with something that
might happen in the future.

– Probably. Fear really helps me to avoid a possible danger.

– You are full of all kinds of possible fears. Your fear of not knowing if you are living your life right is a splendid example. Are you in
any real danger right now, at this moment?

– I guess not.

– But you're still scared. Do you understand what I mean?

I stopped to think of his words for a moment. Maybe he was right.
In fact, I was worried or scared of something all the time whether I
realized it myself or not.

– I do. I worry too much sometimes.

– Worry is fear's best friend. They walk hand in hand, keeping
you on a leash. You have free will. You can listen either to the inner
Voice or to your self. It's up to you to choose. You can do whatever
you want. The Voice will wait for as long as you want to play the
game and walk in the labyrinth.

– What are you actually trying to say? You're talking as if I only
had two choices, and actually only one after all. That can't be freedom!

– You have listened to your self all your life. Now there is one new
choice on the platter. It is still up to you which one you want to listen
to. As long as there's "someone" who chooses, there's also "someone"
who has a free choice. You are the master of your own life, aren't
you?

– Yes, no one else can decide for me. Why do you think I would be
willing to listen to some Voice?

– No one wants to suffer eternally. You too, want to feel Love and be Free.

– But what do love and freedom have to do with the voice?

– That's something you have to find out, the man said smiling broadly.

– The Voice wants you to do what you Love. The self wants you to feel guilt and a bunch of different kinds of fears.

– I don't think that anyone wants to feel guilt or fear intentionally.

– That's right. No-one wants that, people just listen to themselves.

– Do you really mean that I can do only what I love? And there's nobody to judge me? I asked hopefully.

– Yes. There's no one to judge your decisions but yourself.

– That is amazing news! I exclaimed enthusiastically. Provided, of course, that it's true.

– You have to find out. There's no other way. Concentrate on what you really Love. The more you Love, the more you can feel Love. And the more you can feel Love, the more you can Love.

– That sounds awfully beautiful, I sighed.

– The bubble will burst at some stage. Don't let guilt and fear stand in your way. You need courage and determination to be able to listen to the Voice.

– Now you're again talking as if I was going into a battle.

– The self doesn't easily give in. You just have to trust Life.

– Yes, life is very interesting after all. And it's so nice talking to you. I'm really grateful to have met you. I said with a shy smile.

– It's been a pleasure talking to you. And thank Life for everything. Love has its own ways, the man said smiling, and there was no timidness in his smile.

– I feel a lot better now. I've been crying lately, more than ever before. I think it's done me a lot of good since I don't usually cry easily.

– Just let all the emotions appear as they do.

– So many memories keep coming into my mind and so many things to think about. As if a bottle of champagne had popped open.

– That describes your situation excellently. All things you haven't been aware of come rushing into your consciousness. The less you try to control your thoughts the more easily they pop up in your consciousness freely. It is very important just to let everything come, but it's just as important to let everything go. The self is in panic and anxious to grab every thought it has been trying to hide from you. You will analyze and contemplate everything a lot. You don't want to let go.

– That's absolutely right. That's why I came to see you again.

– I'm very glad you came. If a thought is bothering you it's no use denying it. You have to take it, put it on the table in front of you and examine it at leisure. After you have stared at it eye to eye for some time you can let it go. As I said, don't cling to anything.

– Yeah. I'll try. I feel much better now after talking to you.

– Life helps you in many incredible ways. You just have to be ready, open and willing to receive all the help you can get. I want to emphasize once more, don't let the fear take you over. When you trust, Life will surely help you. When you trust you will, little by little, come to see what I mean.

– So I just have to have the courage to face all my fears.

– Exactly. You have to trust Life. You won't dare to face your fears unless you trust Life. You have to let go of everything.

– Let go of everything? I was getting a bit nervous again.

– Yes, we have already talked about your need to have everything under control, in other words the need of the self to keep a hold on you.

– That's right, I said, as my restlessness grew.

– Observe which part of you wants to control. It wants to control everything: your thoughts, other people, life in general – just absolutely everything. The self doesn't want every thought to just come and go, neither does it want to let go and be moved by Life. The self wants to cling and control. It wants to decide what you think and how you live. You only have to become aware of this part in you. Once again, you don't have to do anything to it. It is enough that you become aware of that part in you, and then leave it alone. The self cannot control you if you don't let it do so. You have free will.

– So I am not allowed to decide anything myself any more.

– Sure you are, but then you continue walking in the labyrinth. Only the inner Voice will help you out of the labyrinth. The self wants only to lead you deeper into it.

– That sounds distressing, I said, a little scared.

– That's for sure. That's exactly what the self wants, it wants you to be afraid. It develops all kinds of thoughts which have meanings that cause suffering, so that it can have a firm hold on you. The self is making all kinds of obstacles in front of you, which you have to overcome. Fear is the most difficult one.

– I don't know if I agree with you on what you said about fear. I don't think that fear is always an obstacle. Sometimes it's like a safety wall that helps you avoid a possible danger, I insisted with raised voice. I felt the need to defend.

– Listen to yourself. Fear is like a safety wall, the man repeated calmly – It's exactly this part in you that you shouldn't listen to. Just let it explain, let it kind of talk to itself. You don't have to do what it says.

– I don't agree. You can't manage in life if you don't try. My need to defend just kept on growing. I was ready to argue with the man.

The man didn't, however, say anything. We were both quiet for a while. I felt very uneasy and wanted to escape from the situation as soon as possible. How was it possible that the interesting conversation had turned out to be so harassing? Raindrops began falling from the sky – first one or two here and there, then more and more until the rain made the ground thunder.

– I have to go. I've got to go and take the washing down. I used the rain as an excuse to get away from the situation.

– All right, the man answered calmly.

– Let's talk more some other time.

– That's fine, the man smiled warmly.

I ran into the rain. I wanted to go away, far away. I wanted to go somewhere, anywhere. Anywhere but here.

13

Courage
— fear is just a feeling

In the evening I couldn't sleep. My thoughts were bouncing once again from one thing to another. I pondered everything I had discussed with the man. I felt somehow insecure – Something was making me nervous. I kept sighing because I didn't understand what was wrong with me. Why had I behaved so irrationally? What had gotten into me? The man only wanted to help me, or at least that was what he said. I noticed I was having an inner conversation; I was having a conversation with myself.

Suddenly I realized I was criticising myself. I was playing the game. And that was exactly what I wasn't supposed to do. I was supposed to just observe, neutrally observe. I don't have to do anything, I just have to let things be, I explained to myself. That's it! I'm really talking to myself. This thought stopped me. For a while my thoughts stopped, the thinker stopped. I had realized something, I just didn't understand what. I continued the conversation with myself. For an instant I saw myself, but because I couldn't separate Myself from the thinker, I didn't understand what I had realized. I identified myself with the thinker and not with That that watches the thinker. So I continued thinking. I tried to be neutral and let the thoughts just roll on, but it was difficult, really difficult. It was difficult because I myself was trying to be neutral.

The next day I went to meet the man again. I felt that we hadn't been able to finish our conversation because I had wanted to leave. And I had left. But now I wanted to talk a bit more about fear because there was something in this whole thing that baffled me. Luckily the man was alone in front of his tent.

– Hi, again, I said with a faint smile.

– Well, hello, he answered smiling back at me.

– I'm sorry I left so abruptly yesterday.

– You don't have to be sorry about anything. You haven't done anything wrong.

– Oh yes, there's no right or wrong, I muttered more to myself than to him.

– Just sit down. I don't think you only came to apologize.

– How did you guess? I said with relief and sat down beside the man, or rather beside my friend for he felt like a friend, a real friend to me. He really wasn't a person who got stuck in the past. – It's true that I'd like to continue our conversation about fear and being afraid in general. I don't think I was very attentive yesterday.

– Oh yes, you were. Otherwise you wouldn't be here today. There's nothing wrong in being afraid. It's enough to observe which part of you is afraid and to not let this part take you over. Don't let that fearing part order what you do. This part that feels fear, your self, tries to have a firm grip of you by developing that fear.

– That's exactly what bothers me. I can't help worrying all the time. The future, for example, seems so uncertain at times. By planning my life I try to prevent..., I couldn't finish my sentence.

– Exactly…a new fear again. The self wants you to listen to it, it doesn't want you to let go. It tries to control everything till the very end. By controlling it makes you feel temporarily safe, the safety you already Have. The self tries to look for something that you already Have. You don't feel safe because it is this very need to look for security that makes you uncertain. By striving to control everything the self makes you imagine that you are able to control your own future or anything else that causes you uncertainty. The self doesn't want you to know that the security it offers is only a pale reflection of what real security Is. If you knew what you really Are you couldn't be afraid of the future or anything else, come to that.

– Really?! It is hard for me to imagine life without fear. Aren't you then ever afraid of anything?

– Never. I Am completely safe. Nothing can ever harm Me. There is no one any more who could cause insecurity. There is no one anymore to be afraid.

– That does sound interesting, I said. I would have liked to say daring, but there was nothing defiant in the man. He didn't really seem to act the role of a movie hero, or any other role. I couldn't imagine that he would do extreme jumps only to show others or himself something. He didn't seem to have a need to perform anything. He just was, sincerely just was.

– Before you face all of your fears, you can't know what I mean. Fear is just a feeling, nothing else. It can't control you if you can see through it.

– Somehow you make fear seem so simple and insignificant. To me fear is the worst possible feeling ever and very difficult to face. And all the fears don't even have anything to do with me. I'm afraid of losing Jani, my family and my friends. If I had children, I would probably be crazy with fear and worry all the time. But there's no way I could protect everyone all the time, even if I could protect myself.

– I'm not saying that it would be easy to face one's fears. I'm not belittling the influence of fear on you. The self does everything it can to prevent you from listening to the Voice. It is awfully clever in developing different kinds of fears. The self knows you, and because of this it knows the best ways to make you afraid. All the fears are always connected with you yourself. You worry about your loved ones because you feel they are part of you. As we spoke earlier, your identity includes all the people and things that are close to you. We also talked about groups and everything you feel you own, in other words, your need to belong to something as part of it. All the people and other things that you feel are part of you are also part of your self, your identity. You identify yourself with everything that begins with my or our. When a person who is connected with you suffers, you suffer too. You identify yourself with the group you regard as your own, and the most important group is usually your family and other people close to you. If you knew what the people belonging to this group really Are you couldn't feel any fear for them. You would know that nothing could ever hurt them. They are always safe – just as you are too. But that's what you don't understand yourself.

– But all the pain and suffering is true for them too. And if they die I won't ever see them again.

– I understand what you mean. But if you knew, really knew, not only on the level of thought, you would be certain that nothing can ever hurt them. You couldn't suffer because of them. But of course, this isn't possible until you know what you and all your loved ones really Are.

– Well, that sounds relieving in principle.

– But, my purpose is not to make you lean on any thought. The only way out of suffering is to find out what you really Are. After that, all thoughts will be insignificant. Then you know.

– I really do want to know. I don't want to be afraid any more, not for myself or anybody else.

14

Determination

Our conversation had acquired a more profound tone than earlier, or perhaps it began to gradually dawn on me what the man really wanted to say.

– You need determination, the man said firmly. – You have to really want to know; more than anything else, you have to really want to know.

This challenge woke my inner lion up.

– That's exactly what I want. I do want to know! And I really meant it. I felt a burning need to know what life was all about.

– This journey is never easy for anybody. Are you ready for everything that might appear on your journey?

– Have you ever met anyone else from Finland? Do you know what "sisu" means? I asked, full of determination.

– Well, I don't know yet what it means but I have a funny feeling that I will soon find out, the man said, slightly amused.

– You know, from childhood we Finns are fed "sisu" every morning with our breakfast porridge. Without it you just can't survive in life. Without "sisu" we couldn't, for example, manage the winter. Do you know anything about the Finnish winter?

– No, I don't.

– It's cold and dark, re-al-ly cold and dark. The temperature can drop lower than minus thirty degrees centigrade, and it is only light for a few hours daily. And when I say light, I don't mean sunshine but a faint glimmer in the horizon. Midwinter in northern Finland you can't even see the glimmer, it's grey or dark, day and night. Can you imagine? I looked at the man questioningly for a moment and took a deep breath. – Did you know that we Finns have fought the Russians? Do you know where Russia is? My voice was rising even more.

– I know where Russia is.

– That giant state tried to take the independence of our little country. But no! They didn't succeed! And do you know why?

The man didn't say anything.

– Because we Finns have "sisu"! And guess what game is sacred to us Finns? I too had played that game for years.

The man remained quiet.

– Ice hockey. You can never guess what you need to play that game! Have you ever watched it played?

The man was still sitting without saying a word.

– Well, "sisu", of course! And you probably can guess already what I have needed during this whole year. Do you think that living in a van is easy? We don't even have a toilet, let alone a shower.

The man sat still and didn't open his mouth. I became aware of my agitation and fell into a slightly embarrassed silence. I felt a bit ill at ease. We both sat there for a while without saying anything, because the man was clearly waiting for me to calm down before continuing the conversation.

– You don't need defiance to be determined. Defiance comes from the need to attack or defend. You're not going into a war – you're not going to win anything. The self wants to wage war and win. You are going towards peace.

– Well, I don't really want to go to war. I just wanted you to know that I don't give up very easily.

– I understand. You will need your "sisu", the man laughed good-naturedly. – But defiance you need to let go. It is very important for you to recognise what part in you feels the need to attack and defend. This part wants you to go on fighting. War between countries is just a collective reflection of your self. You don't have to literally take up arms to be able to attack or defend. You are continuously at war with your environment, that is yourself, anyway.

– What do you mean? Continuously at war?

– The self preserves its existence by attacking and defending. You attack or defend every time you feel threatened, in other words, every time you feel afraid. The self wants to survive.

– It's true that I defend myself, I said, feeling a bit embarrassed.

– The self defends everything it identifies itself with: body, family, country, team, religion, opinion, image and so on. Defending occurs not only during wars or "playful" games but also for example, by wanting to always be right. Defending can also appear as submission, denial, sacrifice, and argumentation. Sometimes it is a conscious act, sometimes it isn't. We have already discussed the self's defense forces. Defending is connected with your need to control and dominate.

I examined the man closely, trying to make him see that I was really trying to understand what he said, and that I wouldn't digest everything just like that.

– Attacking also is connected with the actions of the defense forces, he continued. Defending and attacking are interconnected. As I said, you feel the need to attack when you feel threatened. By attacking you defend yourself. Attacking comes out as the need to be right or arguing and quarrelling, but also as deliberate provocation, threatening, subjugation, the need for recognition, purposeful damaging, and hatred in general. The need to win is also connected with the need to attack. By winning the self believes it has defeated the threat. After you have won, the threat is over and the self is safe. Revenge is closely connected with attacking as well. With revenge the self tries to patch up the threatened part of itself. One might feel that one is a victim of injustice, and then want to take revenge in order to patch up the hole one has made oneself. By taking revenge the self makes you believe that you can recover something you've lost. You can't stand the feeling of loss because you want to feel complete, whole. By taking revenge, you are searching for a piece

that is missing from your puzzle, and don't want to wake up to realize that there is no puzzle after all. There has never been one, you
just believe there is.

– Oh! Interesting! Go on.

– The self uses the body when it's attacking or defending. By observing your body, in other words yourself, you can find out how the
need to attack and defend is expressed in you. That takes us back to
objective observation. The purpose is not to find the culprit, but to
see, without criticizing or judging, how the self acts to preserve its
existence. Every time you feel the need to attack or defend yourself,
or notice that you have already begun to do so, try to see why you
are acting the way you are. Ask yourself what it is that you are trying to defend. What you are trying to defend doesn't really exist. It is
just an illusion – you only believe it exists.

As I couldn't argue his point I just stared at him intently.

– You need willpower, firm determination, not to let the self take
control in you. The self does everything in its power to persuade you
to join the war. It's easy to join a fight but refusing to wage war de-
mands determination. And I'm not talking about submission, resig-
nation, or sacrifice when I talk about refusing. I'm not asking you to
submit yourself to anything, resign yourself to anything or sacrifice
yourself for anything. If you have those feelings, find out what in
you submits, gives up or sacrifices itself. The self is cunning. It takes
advantage of every means available.

– So I just have to observe myself, is that it?

– That's right – and stop obeying orders. Stop doing what the self
tells you to do. Take the body back from your self.

– Sounds pretty wild. As if a beast lives inside of me.

– You can describe the self in any way you feel is appropriate. The
most important thing is to stop obeying it. You need strong determination to be able not to act as the self wants you to act.

– It does sound interesting and challenging but I'm still not quite
sure yet what it means in practice.

– Don't worry about that. If you are alert you will soon find out.
And I'd like to emphasize once more that determination doesn't re-
quire any trying or any defiance. Determination, in fact, is effortless.

It is only when the self decides something and wants to get this something that you have to take pains.

– I see.

– This may sound a bit confusing but it is important for you to be aware that you don't have to get anywhere or achieve anything. You don't have to do anything or be anything to be able to know what you Are. You already have what you're looking for. You already are what you Are.

I know now that many people who consider themselves seekers or persons on the spiritual path believe that certain kinds of rituals and rites will help them to achieve something that may be called enlightenment, for example. The self is really cunning. But you don't have to be able to stand on your head, follow a certain diet or sit on a hill for years to be able to know your real Being. By changing external circumstances one only works on one's identity. You don't have to change anything in yourself. Changing your life or your self can in no way affect what you really Are. This doesn't mean that you can't or won't change your life. Your life is what it is. More important is to dig even deeper.

15

There is no time

I looked at the man for a while, and remained quiet. It was no surprise that my thoughts were once more bouncing here and there. I tried to catch one and examine it closer but for some reason I couldn't manage to do that. I was floating in the middle of questions and answers but wasn't able to pair them sensibly.

  – I'm quite baffled. I really do want to understand what you are trying to explain but I don't know what I should think. On the one hand, I feel there's nothing to be done. Like you said, nothing has to change. But on the other hand, I feel that something's got to change anyway. I can't even explain what I mean. I just have a vague feeling that there's something in my way. It's as if you were explaining something very simple but I just can't grasp it.

  – Don't worry. All you need is patience. Life is an ongoing process —some of the changes just seem to happen faster, others more slowly. Something indeed has to change because everything is changing constantly. I can understand that this may sound conflicting to you. Nothing has to change but still everything is changing. We are now talking about time which in reality doesn't exist at all. Change always occurs in time. Everything seems to change but in reality nothing ever changes. Change is an illusion and appears only in connection with time. What you Are never changes. It can never change because It is not part of time. You yourself have a past and a future but what you really Are just Is.

– What do you mean? You say there's no time. Even right at this moment time is passing.

– Time passes only for your self. You identify yourself with time and preserve your existence with the help of time. Without time you yourself wouldn't even exist.

– How come?

– All your life is composed of time: you are spinning your story with the help of time. What would you be if you didn't have a past and a future?

– I guess I'd be dead.

– Right. Your self would be dead.

– But even if I died myself, life would go on. Life existed before I was even born, I insisted.

– You're talking about time now. The past is nothing but a bunch of images and memories. Time moves on the basis of different meanings. Even your future is composed of images you have created yourself. Time preserves its existence using thoughts which are images composed of meanings. Time is only a line of images. Time is thought.

– Time is only a thought? I asked incredulously.

– Yes, it is, just as you are yourself. All your identity is composed of images, thoughts that you believe are true. The man paused for a while to give me time to digest what he had just said. – There's nothing else than this moment, the now-moment. Everything occurs in this moment. All your past happened now, and all your possible future will happen now. You yourself don't perceive the present moment because the self is building a bridge over it. Right now the self is building a bridge from the basis of the past. The self sees this moment in the light of the past, and in the light of the past it builds the future. Your thoughts are always either about the past or the future – or about the present built on the past. The self Is never Now. The self can never Be Now, for it needs time to survive.

Little by little the man's words began to make sense to me. Something in me was clearly waking up, or I was getting used to the way he talked.

– You identify yourself as a person living in time. You believe you are a person living your own life, in other words, acting a role in a play based on time. You believe you are a person who lives, a person who acts on the stage. You believe you were born on the stage, and on the stage you will die too. If you were able to watch your life from aside, like a spectator at a performance, you would recognize what you really Are. You are not an actor performing on the stage and living your life. You are now, a spectator watching a performance based on time, your life.

– Do you mean that I am acting in some performance?

– Yes, I do, in a theatre performance called life.

– Life is only a theatre performance? I was getting worried again. A strange restlessness spread over me. The man had compared life with a theatre performance before but I hadn't given it a second thought. Somehow the idea seemed natural in a peculiar way, but on the other hand, it frightened me.

– Yes, it is, and you're very serious when you are acting in it. Your role is very personal to you.

– But I'm not acting. I don't have the need to perform anything, not with you anyway.

– I think you are now talking about role plays on the stage. At this moment you are not in a place where you would feel the need to perform a role consciously. You are acting both consciously and unconsciously. The conscious role includes manners, for instance. In that case the actors have made a mutual agreement as to how to behave on the stage. However, you are acting all the time even if you don't realize it yourself; Sanna lives even if she doesn't try to perform anything. The play goes on even if the main actor isn't aware of it.

– Am I the actor performing the main role?

– Yes, you are, you yourself.

– Wow! Sounds wild! But I don't want to act in any performance, not as the main actor anyway.

– You aren't. You just believe you are.

– Excuse me? You just said that I'm playing a role, even if I wasn't aware of it myself.

– The play is based on time, and time is only an illusion. When you perceive you're watching a play, you can either go on watching or walk out of the whole theatre. After all, there is no-one to watch the play. The moment of now needs neither a past nor a future, the moment of now isn't even here.

– There we go again, I just don't get it, I said shaking my head.

– It's all right. The most important thing is that you concentrate on this moment as well as you can. I am aware that you said earlier that it's quite impossible for you to concentrate on this moment, which I think is a significant observation. It means that you are aware of how the self is building a bridge on the present moment. The self doesn't give in very easily. It needs time to preserve its existence. The self knows how to use force and it has a will of its own. It can lose its power only through your awareness. By concentrating on the present moment you are demolishing the bridge the self is building. The bridge will break down sooner or later – it can't not. You just need determination.

– So I just have to try to keep my thoughts in the present moment, is that it?

– You don't have to try anything. It's enough to observe your thoughts neutrally without judging. By observing, you will find out how the self works. The self wants you to regurgitate and ruminate on the past using the hooks "what if" and "I should have". It survives with the help of the past. The self makes you feel guilt, shame, remorse, bitterness, disappointment and hatred, for example. None of these feelings would be possible without your identification with the past. The self is cunning. The past doesn't count. It is only yourself that gives it meaning. You're not an actor performing a role, and none of the other actors on the stage have done anything else than perform a role, a role that makes no difference. You can take the past from your shoulders and put it down. The self does not want you to do that. When you listen to the self the past is reflected into the present moment as well. The past blurs your sight, and you can't see then how everything Is in this moment – Now. For example, you are not able to See what I Am in reality, you only see the story of me you have made up yourself. By using time, you compose a story of different images that you believe in, that you believe is me.

– What do you mean?

– Using your memories, your mental images, you have formed a conception of me. You have developed a character for the stage. You have created an actor you believe in on the basis of your own opinions and observations. You see a person with various characteristics, an individual with a body.

– That's true. I do have a certain kind of picture of you in my mind.

– Your self began to develop an idea of what I'm like from the moment we met. This idea of the self is always based on illusion since it's real only to your self. You only see the shell that the self has built using time as an instrument, and this shell has nothing to do with what I really Am.

– Mmm... interesting, I said scrutinizing the man from head to toe.

– The images are formed automatically, and there's nothing wrong with that. It is enough to notice how the self works. I am not what you think I am.

It is true that we keep on forming images and conceptions of everything and everyone without being aware of it. This is how the self works, and this is how it survives. The self is a system that automatically feeds and recreates itself all the time. This is exactly why it's essential to step aside to make observations of the process instead of identifying with it and imagining that it's all there is. This mis-identification cannot be solved on the level at which it was created; the problem of the self cannot be solved on the level of the self.

– As I already said, the man continued, the self also creates images of the future by making use of the past. The self wants you to plan and consider the future. The self craves for different future objectives and feeds you with its "some day" instrument. The self wants you to live in the future, not in the present. It doesn't want you to face this moment as it Is. The self wants to give you hope and hold you in the grip of fear. All your future images have originated in fear. You are thinking of the future because you are afraid. You don't have the courage to let yourself plunge into the present because you can't bear the uncertainty that is caused by concentrating in the present. You are afraid to give up control and let Life lead. You don't trust Life, you only trust yourself. You need the bridge that gives you the imaginary feeling of security. We already discussed the need of the self to seek security, the security that you already Have. Remember?

– Yes, I do.

– The self makes your future safe using different means it has invented. A very good example of this is money. Money brings the feeling of security to many people, but what happens when the money is lost?

– Yes, I see.

– The feeling of security that money brings is only as strong as a house of cards. The self also seeks security by owning things and belonging to different groups. This makes the self feel safe. By owning and belonging to something, the self wants to secure the future.

– Do you mean that I shouldn't own anything or belong to anything any more?

– No, I don't. Nothing external matters if you don't identify yourself with it. It is enough that you observe why you are doing what you are doing. Observe why you feel the need to plan and in general secure your future. Observe what it is in you that is afraid. By planning and securing your future, you only try to hide your fear. With the help of the future you don't have to face your fear. Do you know what I mean?

I didn't think I did, so I kept quiet.

– The self doesn't want you to face your biggest fear, the fear which initiates all the other fears, the fear that everything ends. You are afraid of dying, and because you are afraid of dying, you are also afraid that everyone who is part of you – everyone close to your self – will die too.

– Yes, that's right. I don't want to die, and I really don't want anyone close to me to die either.

– You connect death with the body, and as long as the body functions you believe you're alive. Your future continues as long as the body survives. Time and body are tightly connected with each other.

– Just a minute, can you repeat that?

– Your future continues as long as the body survives. Time and body are tightly connected with each other. With the help of the body you count your age. By taking advantage of the body the self continues making up your story based on time. For example, you celebrate your birthday with the help of the body. Body is part of time, and by using time you count your age. The self divides time into parts, just as it does with everything else. The calendar, the clock and your age are all born because of that.

– Yes, I'm twenty-nine, I said with a smile.

– Because you identify yourself with your body – and the body is not permanent like everything else connected with time – you believe you will die. The self uses the body to make you believe in your own birth and death. As long as the body functions it gives you a future. Most people have to face death only when their body is getting old and nears the end of its life. But you can die before the body stops functioning. The self uses the body as long as it can.

– What?! I can die before I die? What's that?

– The death you believe in isn't actually a death at all. The real death means the death of the self, not your death. You can never die. As I've repeated many times the self only uses the body to preserve its own existence. You believe you are alive.

– That's what you keep saying but I just don't get it.

– The self doesn't die when the body dissolves. It only uses the body to survive. You believe your self and think you're alive. The self takes advantage of the body and keeps you in the belief of being alive as long as the body keeps functioning. Using the body, the self makes you feel afraid. It makes you feel afraid of the dissolution of your body, your idea of death. The self survives by maintaining this fear.

– I still don't understand this.

– The self has developed a fear according to which you will die. The fear of death helps the self to preserve its existence. You are afraid of not being. The fear of not being makes you fear death. The self wants to exist. It doesn't want to die. You believe in the fear the self has developed. The self does everything in its power to preserve its existence. It even creates a fear to make you believe in itself.

– Are you trying to say that the fear of death is just a sham?

– Exactly. The self has developed this fear to make you feel afraid. Using this fear it makes you obedient.

– Maybe so but the fear of death is quite concrete to me.

– Of course it is: that's exactly what the self wants.

– Do you mean that death itself is a sham too?

– Yes. It's just a splendid way the self has discovered to stay alive.

– I really don't know what to think, I sighed, shaking my head.

– There are a lot of other fears too that are connected with the future. The fear of death is just the leader of all the other fears. Without the leader, there wouldn't be any other fears.

– Do I have to question all my fears, then?

– Yes, each and every one of them. All fears are born from yourself.

– I still don't fully get what you mean by the self, there is something in all of this that baffles me.

– Just observe your thoughts. That's enough. The self cannot hide itself forever.

– So, I will never die, and time is just an illusion?

– That's right, but don't get stuck in thoughts of immortality and the non-existence of time. The self is cunning.

– That means that instead of just wanting to believe I have to find out for myself. Is that it?

– Great! That's it exactly. The thought is always behind. The Truth will only be revealed now, now, now... Life is now, not yesterday or tomorrow.

16

What everybody is looking for

The man stretched his arms and lay down on his back. After a while I did the same. The sky was beautiful, the sun was shining and the clouds were slowly moving across the sky. A warm serenity spread over me. We lay on the grass for quite a while without speaking, listening to the sounds around us, until my patience ran out and I sat up.

– Can you explain a little more what you meant by the role characters? You think that I'm acting a role, and have even developed one for you. Something in this thought bothers me and I can't get it out of my mind.

– I understand, the man said, sitting up too. – I was talking about the shell which you have built yourself using time. Without a shell the actor is unable to perform his role. The shell is composed of many parts, and the most important of them is the body. People pay a lot of attention to the body and the outward appearance in general these days. The self wants you to believe that you are what you look like. For many, the body is the most important of role costumes because it has been given the most meaning. Do you understand what I mean?

Yeah, I nodded timidly.

– The importance of the body comes of course from the identification with it. You can clearly see in the environment how important looks are. Every one of us has a picture of what we should look like.

– Oh yes, I know what you mean, I said, sighing deeply.

– The more important the outward appearance is the more one identifies oneself with it. You feel you are more than or less than, better than or worse than, depending on what you think you look like. It makes, however, no difference what you think you look like since it isn't what you really Are. What you really Are can shine through the shell but you are by no means the shell.

I glanced at him. A shell? What shell? I wondered.

– The shell isn't only the body, it also includes everything that the actor considers part of itself outwardly. In addition to the body, it also includes your residence, car, job, clothes, family, circle of friends, hobbies plus everything else that has meaning externally. They are all part of one's shell or appearance. Everything external that has any importance to the person is part of the props that the actor needs for his role. The more important the prop becomes, the more you identify yourself with it. With the help of the props, you show what you are.

– Oh, I see. The shell, in fact, is everything that others can see of us, and on the other hand, everything we want to show to others.

– Exactly. The shell is the instrument that makes acting possible. Different achievements are often also part of the shell. Appearance and achievements are generally the most significant features that people want to know about an actor when creating the role character. The achievements give a picture of what the person is. Any thought is sufficient as long as the actor plays the role using it. The self never feels it is sufficient and therefore tries to cover this unpleasant feeling with achievements. By achieving something you get the feeling you are enough – or even something more. The more you identify with your achievements, the more they mean to you. The achievements usually define the direction to which the actor on the stage is moving. Whatever the achievement is, the idea is to reach for or preserve something. Without achievements the person feels inadequate and a failure. The self doesn't want you to know the secret that you are already enough. You don't have to achieve anything to be perfect.

– Yes, you said earlier that I'm perfect. It's just that the idea seems so alien to me. Somehow, I'm used to thinking that nothing is ever enough for myself or for anyone else. One should always strive for something more.

– Remember it's enough that you observe what you're doing. There's nothing wrong in pursuing a goal. The most important thing is that you understand that nothing you can achieve will ever be enough for you permanently – and while it seems to be enough you are constantly afraid of losing it. The need to achieve always originates in fear. You're afraid you aren't enough. You're afraid you can't reach your goal or that you will lose it. By trying to achieve something you can't wake up to realize what you really Are.

– I'm really relieved to hear that I don't have to do or change anything. It's wonderful if I'm enough as I am.

– Love makes you Free, it doesn't chain you.

– How nice it would be to be able to fly up there like that bird, I said pointing at the sky.

– What you really Are is always Free.

– Something stops me from being free. Could you tell me something more about the shell that I've made for myself?

My question brought a warm smile on the man's lips because he saw that my curiosity had clearly been awoken.

– Because you identify yourself with the body you also identify yourself with your gender. You believe you are a woman.

– Are you going to tell me next that I'm not a woman after all? I giggled, about to blush.

– Yes, I am. But that is naturally connected with the fact that you are not a body.

– Yeah, that's right. Good that you made that point quite clear, I said smiling to myself, because I knew very well that he didn't mean that I looked like a man.

– The actors have created numerous roles that have something to do with gender. I'm talking about conscious roles now, role plays such as manners, for instance, that I have already mentioned. According to

these gender roles you should behave in a way that is characteristic
of your gender. We are taught these roles when we are very young.
Girls are brought up to be women and boys to be men. Gender is very
important to your identity.

– It sure is. I'm a woman. I said with a blink of the eye.

– In fact, you only believe you're a woman, and because you believe that, you behave in a way a woman should. Women have their
own roles and men theirs.

– I see what you mean. The woman does the washing up and the
man fixes the car.

– That's right.

– But these roles are changing today, at least in western countries.
Equality is becoming more and more important these days.

– Well, the roles are changing all the time depending on the society and the era. The most important thing for you to understand is
that you don't have to behave in the way your gender should behave
according to the dominant opinion. The self only tries to keep you on
the leash.

– I think I understand what you mean, but aren't some of the roles
quite natural? Girls are girls and boys are boys.

– What is natural to you?

– The kind of behaviour that doesn't feel forced.

– Exactly. You mean a role that you aren't forced to try and perform
consciously.

– Maybe. I still don't really understand how I am acting without
realizing it myself, I groaned.

– All role plays on the stage are just that, role plays. If you don't
want to take on a role, just quit. If you want to act a role, go on acting it. You are free to choose. You don't have to act any role you don't
want to. In fact, you don't have to act anything but the roles you Love.
And now I'm talking about all the roles, not only those that have
something to do with gender.

– So, I am really just acting?! That's extremely difficult to grasp.

– Yes, you are acting. Everything is just a play. That is why I encourage you to observe why you're acting in the way you are. Most
of the role plays originate in fear. Identification with different roles

brings safety. We have already discussed your need to belong. You don't want to feel different, separate. Being different frightens you. When you belong you feel safe. In other words, by behaving according to the role models that are generally accepted, even admired, you feel you are accepted and secure.

– So I just have to question all my actions?

– Yes. Just concentrate on what you really Love.

– Oh, how lovely it would be if everyone was allowed to do what they really want to do.

– But everyone is allowed to do what they really want to do.

– Yes, yes, but I mean all kinds of discrimination. For many people, for example, their appearance or gender is an obstacle to what they'd like to do.

– Could you explain more specifically what you mean? The man asked trying very clearly to make me state the reasons for my opinions.

– Well, dark-skinned people, for instance, are discriminated against because of their skin colour, and homosexuals because of their sexual orientation. It isn't very easy to be different on this planet.

– Remember that the environment is only a reflection of yourself. The self is always different and only by identifying itself with a certain group can it hide this difference and the feeling of separateness. Being different, however, helps an individual to dig deeper than the surface, so in that respect everyone who feels themselves different is lucky.

– What an interesting point of view!

– You are not your appearance or your sexuality. You Are something much more miraculous.

– I don't think that helps anyone who feels they are being discriminated against.

– Maybe it does, maybe it doesn't. No one is what they think they are anyway.

– Why do homosexuals then believe they're homosexuals? I asked trying to put him in a tight spot for once.

– For the same reason you believe you are heterosexual. The self does anything to preserve its existence.

– Many people believe that it's more natural to be heterosexual than homosexual.

– Yes, many people do really believe that.

– Do you mean that at the end of the day sexuality makes no difference at all?

– Nothing makes any difference. Only Love Is.

– Only love is! Sounds awfully beautiful. I wish everybody thought so.

– It's no use worrying about the others. Just concentrate on yourself and remember that the environment really is nothing but a reflection of your self.

I sighed deeply again. I began to feel that was all I could do. Nevertheless, the thought of love being the only thing that mattered felt very attractive and genuine in my heart of hearts. I was hoping that we would take up this topic once again later but didn't have the courage to talk about it right then.

– Discrimination is really interesting, I said just to keep the conversation going.

– Being different frightens you. You don't want to admit what you really feel. By being discriminatory towards others you project your feeling of separateness outside yourself. You try to make that feeling be something outside of yourself, something separate from you. You're afraid of what you are.

– Do you mean that by discriminating I try to deny something, that discrimination is just another way to hide feelings?

– Yes. To be more exact, by discriminating you try to hide what you feel you are. You don't want to admit that you feel different and separate yourself.

– I don't think there's anything to hide in being different. I think it is fascinating. I think it's wonderful that all people are different. There are no two persons exactly alike. Everybody is unique.

– Tolerance and broadmindedness are very important qualities.

The man examined me with his X-ray look. I couldn't help feeling again that I was quite naked and vulnerable but for some reason it didn't make me nervous this time – on the contrary, I felt pleased that someone was looking straight through me.

– I think you are now ready to take the next step, the man began, clearly weighing in his mind what words he should use to go on. – When you reach the Destination you will know that you and everybody else are One. In reality you do not differ from others at all. It is only the self that feels itself separate. All differences are part of the shell.

– People are just shells, like eggshells! I laughed.

– People aren't shells – you only see the shell. As long as you believe that the performance is real, you see thinking bodies, actors performing their roles. You called the shell an eggshell. At this moment you aren't able to see what Is inside it, you just see the shell. You believe you are an egg, but in fact, you are the Chicken. Although this figure of speech is quite naive, it can be used as an example. To be able to know what you really Are the shell must crack. The Chicken inside will not live forever in the shelter provided by the shell, It will crack the shell as soon as you are ready.

I stared at the man. Now I was some kind of chicken! At times the man used really bizarre words and symbols. However, it was true that I saw all people as thinking bodies.

– As long as you feel you're a separate being, your longing to belong, to be part of something remains. In addition to mental longing, the longing also appears physical. Have you ever really thought about why you want to have sex?

– What?

– Why do you want to have sex?

I blushed. My face instantly turned the brightest red. I wasn't used to talking about sex with a strange man. Well, he wasn't so strange to me any more, but still. The question was so sudden.

– Because it..errr.. feels good, I answered uneasily.

– And? he asked encouragingly. He must have noticed my embarrassment but didn't let that disturb him.

– Because of the intimacy. I think it's wonderful to be close to Jani.

– You want to have sex because it feels good and it's intimate. Why does sex feel good and why do you feel this intimacy?

– Ah...well...you know...the orgasm? At this stage I think even my toenails were glowing red and I could very well have hidden in a strawberry patch.

– I know what an orgasm is, he said and seemed quite relaxed.

– It feels awfully good and liberating, I stammered.

– Yes, exactly – the freedom. You have to trust completely and let go so that you can surrender into sex. Sexual intercourse is a very intimate experience. Therefore it may be a difficult topic to discuss. Do you understand what I mean?

– Yes, I do. During intercourse you have to let another person come very close, and not only physically.

– All defending has to stop. Is that what you mean by intimacy? The man asked.

– I guess so. Intimacy is very important to me although I know that many people have sex just for physical enjoyment.

– People have sex for many different reasons, and one of them is the need to let go. Let's concentrate on that now. What happens during an orgasm? What happens to your self?

I glanced at the man smiling timidly. I still felt quite embarrassed, but didn't feel so uncomfortable any more. I could see that he really wanted to discuss the subject thoroughly.

– The good feeling grows and grows until you reach the climax and everything explodes, I gave a little laugh. – I don't seem to find quite the right words to describe it.

– Sex is energy. Physically the orgasm releases the energy accumulated in the body. But what happens to your self?

I glanced again at the man over arched brow.

– Well, I just told you.

– You said that everything explodes. You were talking about the moment the energy in your body is released. What else?

– I don't quite understand what you are getting at.

– What happens to thoughts while you are making love, and particularly when you are near the climax? And during the climax?

– At that moment I just don't have any time to think at all.

– Exactly. You are Free from your self. There are no thoughts.

– Wow! That's interesting.

– Making love gives you an opportunity to peer into Freedom. You let everything go, literally everything. You let go of yourself – you put your sack down for a while. Besides the intimacy and the physical feeling of togetherness, making love may touch one even deeper. Then the Oneness is something else other than what you can experience through the shell. You want to get even closer to another being than your body allows you to. If you are ready to let go you can get closer, and then even closer still – and in the end…where? What's left when there is no body anymore, when there are no bodies anymore? What's left when you are not there anymore, when you both are not there anymore?

– We-e-ll. I couldn't say.

– Everyone is looking for answers to these questions in one way or another. Everybody wants something and is looking for something. This is the reason for constant restlessness. Few people stop to think what that something really is. What are you looking for?

– I don't really know.

– What do you really want? What made you come to the other side of the Earth?

– You mean, why I wanted to set off on this journey. Is that it?

– I mean what are you looking for? What is everyone on this planet looking for in one way or another?

– Well, I don't quite understand the question.

– Just give yourself a moment to think about it.

I racked my brain for some time and managed in the end to form a fairly sensible thought.

– Do you mean freedom? I asked hopefully.

– What does freedom mean to you?

– That you can do whatever you want.

– Do you think that you are free?

– Well I am and I am not. I consider myself rather lucky.

– When are you free?

– When I can do what I want, which, of course, isn't always possible.

– So freedom comes and goes.

– Yes. Sometimes I feel free, sometimes I don't.

– Freedom isn't a feeling. You may at times have a feeling of temporary freedom but that doesn't mean you are really Free.

– Well, then I just don't know what you mean.

– Just give yourself time to think about it.

I had a mental wrestling match trying to figure out what the man wanted me to answer. I didn't want him to think I was a total idiot, so I was quite satisfied when another idea began to take shape in my mind.

– Do you mean happiness? Everybody wants to be happy.

– You're getting close. Where do Happiness and Freedom come from?

We were both sitting on the grass without saying anything. I looked at the clouds moving in the sky and pondered what the man might mean. Where do happiness and freedom really come from, I thought to myself. After some time the man looked at his watch and stood up briskly.

– Well, I have to go now. We can continue the conversation some other time.

– Oh, alright. Let's talk later then, I said a little disappointed.

– Bye, the man said and went on his way.

– Bye indeed, I said to myself and waved my hand. But the man was nowhere to be seen anymore.

I was on the point of leaving myself, but then I decided to stay awhile and lay down on the grass. The clouds were slowly moving in the sky, and a warm wind touched my hair. Soon the answer to the man's question was clear as crystal in my mind. Perhaps it had been too obvious. Or maybe I just hadn't wanted to admit it.

17

Patience

More than a week passed. I felt more and more restless day by day. I had a feeling that something was happening. I sensed something that I couldn't explain, even to myself. I just had this feeling looming in the background. Observing my thoughts and behaviour incessantly, I tried to be neutral and not to react to anything. I felt I was trying to tame a wild horse. I was very quiet because I was using all my energy to observe myself. I felt a constant need to react both to my own thoughts and everything else around me. Externally I was calm but inside I felt chaos.

Jani wondered why I didn't say anything. He thought I was behaving a bit strangely, which was quite understandable from his point of view, of course. I had told him about the conversations I had had with the man. In Jani's opinion the man's thoughts had started to sound at least partly interesting, too. But he didn't understand why I took the man's words so seriously. By seriousness he was referring to my firm decision to find out what life was about. He knew from many years' experience that when I decided something I would act accordingly. That was exactly why he was a bit worried. This time I had got it into my head to accomplish something entirely impossible. I disagreed with him, naturally: something in life was amiss, something smelt a bit fishy. I couldn't explain what that something was but I had a burning desire to find out.

The days went by routinely. Our working days were long, and afterwards we either rested in our van or spent the evening with the other campers. I didn't see the man until just before we left for Dunsborough. In Asia we had met a nice Australian couple, and they had asked us to spend Christmas with them. Christmas was coming, the first Christmas away from Finland. I felt a bit sad because I missed Finland very much. Christmas had always been very important to me but now I didn't seem to be in the right mood at all. Darkness, snow, candles and good food belonged to a Finnish Christmas. I also missed the sauna and the company of my family. In Australia the situation was quite the opposite: the weather was getting warmer and we had heard that it was already quite hot on the coast. The last few weeks had been unusually rainy and chilly in south-western Australia, but now the weather was changing here too. Summer was on the way.

I was happy that the weather was getting warmer but I just couldn't seem to get into the mood for Christmas. The days off, however, were more than welcome, and it was wonderful to see our friends again. We had already spent some time with them in Dunsborough before coming to Manjimup. Dunsborough is on the coast, and as we had decided to stay longer in Australia we first tried to get work somewhere near there. As we failed to find any kind of work there we started towards the inland areas, and landed in Manjimup by chance. Or that was what I thought at the time.

We were just packing for our short holiday trip when I noticed the man in front of his tent. I wanted to know where he had been and why he had left me sitting on the grass by myself. I felt I'd been cheated. I told Jani I would be back in a minute and started towards the man.

– Where have you been? I asked almost angrily and without a trace of the objectivity of the last few days.

– Oh, hello, the man answered with a smile.

– Why did you leave so suddenly?

– It was good for you to be by yourself. And I, in other words, my role character, was needed elsewhere. You can't cling to me. Life will help you anyway, he answered calmly.

Of course, you can do whatever you like. It's just that I've been worried. Something is happening and I don't know what that something is. I've been very restless the last few days.

– Have you observed your thoughts?

– Yes, I have, and everything else too. I'm watching every person and situation like a hawk.

– Good. What is the impression you get?

– People behave just as you said they do – and for me it's really challenging not to react to anything. I'm just like everybody else.

– You just need patience.

– Patience?!? Me!? I'm a nervous wreck. The tone of my voice tightened again.

The man just looked at me remaining totally calm, and I could only sigh deeply as I'd done so many times before.

– I'm sorry. I'm really on edge. Sometimes I feel like throwing things around, and that's something I never do. Do you understand what I mean?

– Yes, I do. The man answered in his familiar gentle way.

– My thoughts crisscross from the past into the future and vice versa. It is still very difficult to concentrate on the present moment. I also notice I'm judging everything all the time. I'm playing the game you mentioned without a pause. I'm getting fed up with my own thoughts, and don't trust my own opinions any more. I'm trying to question why I'm thinking the way I am.

– You've taken my advice very seriously, the man said.

– That's what Jani says too.

– Just go on in the same way and be merciful to yourself. You only need patience.

– How can you always be so darn understanding? And so calm? You haven't lost your nerve once although I still don't understand what you are trying to explain. It's completely unbelievable!

– There's no hurry.

– How on earth can you bear me? Where do you get the patience to listen and explain? Not even I can stand myself.

– You just need patience. Life will help you.

– I'm not sure I have so much patience. I want answers – and I want them right away. Something is wrong, but I just don't know what it is. Something confuses me.

– Remember to rest. You need a lot of rest, he said after scrutinising me for quite a while.

– I'm really tired. I've felt tired for a couple of weeks now, and I'm getting used to that state. I've even stayed up very late a couple of nights.

– Listen to your body and rest every time you feel the need.

– We're just leaving for Dunsborough for Christmas since we have a few days off. In fact, I have to go back to Jani now, I said glancing at our van.

– Merry Christmas, the man answered smiling.

– Wonderful Christmas to you too. What will you do for Christmas?

– My role character is staying in this camping area.

– Oh yes, of course, I gave a laugh. – And will your role character be here when I get back?

– Sure, but keep your mind open. You don't need my role character

– Life will help you anyway.

– It was nice seeing you again. I hugged the man and started walking towards our van.

18

Nothing happens by chance

The time in Dunsborough passed quickly. The Australian Christmas is a little different from the Finnish one. We started celebrating Christmas on the morning of Christmas Day. We had a substantial breakfast, drank some sparkling wine, and then opened our presents. Santa Claus had visited the house during the night. There was no rice porridge or Christmas sauna, but I felt good even if I thought I was celebrating a hilarious midsummer rather than Christmas. After the presents had been opened we were off to the beach. There were some other friends and relatives of theirs too, so we all got together to enjoy the sun and the relaxed atmosphere. At first I felt a bit uneasy and self-conscious: the rolls that had gathered around my waist were mocking me. I wondered what on Earth I had been eating day in day out. I felt like a big balloon. But I soon noticed my thoughts and stood up.

– Me and my fat are going swimming now, I said, loudly and cheerfully. I was really having a bellyful of my own thoughts. I wanted to enjoy the beach regardless of the critical voice that echoed in my head. And, after all, it was a wonderful day. We spent several hours on the beach, after which we had a barbecue and stayed up late into the night. It goes without saying that not all Australians celebrate Christmas in the way we did. It was only later that I realized what all holidays and other traditions had meant to me. I understood that a meaning is only just a meaning, nothing else. All of the meanings of things, I had given myself. They only meant to me what I wanted them to mean.

After Christmas we returned to Manjimup and continued to work. We had planned to spend the new year on the coast with our friends again. The days between Christmas and New Year's Eve went by quickly, working long hours. We were also getting our van ready for sale, since we had agreed to sell it soon after new year. We had hung up some for-sale adverts on our way to Dunsborough and back, and had received a couple of phone calls. The next week an interested buyer was supposed to come and take a look at the van. We had decided to sell it because we needed more funds for our journey, and the prospect of driving for hours into the outback wasn't so appealing to us anymore. We had booked air tickets for late January from Perth to Adelaide almost immediately after arriving in Manjimup. Our plan was quite clear: we would sell the van, work another month in Manjimup, after which we would go via Perth to Adelaide and from there along the coast towards Sydney in a rented car. We had planned to stay in Australia for another two months. We had tickets booked for New Zealand in early March.

I felt a bit melancholy because we would soon have to give up our home. The van meant a lot to me. I knew from the first moment that it was exactly what we were looking for: it was love at first sight. A Volkswagen Transporter 1984. To tell the truth, I knew nothing about different makes of cars. It was enough for me to see the retro look of the yellow van and the surfboard and the guitar in the back, in the space which would become our joint living room and bedroom. Well, neither of us could surf, let alone play the guitar, but that didn't bother me at all.

We had been only three days in Australia, in Sydney to be more exact, when we found this van, which was to be our travelling companion from then on. The three of us, "the whole family" spent the first night in a parking hall, after which we had lots of different kinds of experiences together. First we drove from Sydney to Cairns and from Cairns to Uluru; from Uluru we drove to Darwin and from Darwin along the coast to Perth – almost all the way around Australia! The van exceeded itself many, many times, transporting us for thousands of kilometers and offering us shelter whenever we needed it. We took good care of it and gave it everything it needed, including some repairs along the way – every home needs taking care of. Right on the first day we noticed that the speedometer wasn't working. I had quite a fit when I realized it. Some other "small things" we had to repair along the way. Before going into the Outback we examined our whole home really carefully. Only the sliding door on the side – the door to the balcony – still needed some work. Neither Jani nor I had any knowledge about cars; Jani perhaps a little but only very little. We had however managed very well, because every time we needed help, out of nowhere appeared a local MacGyver who took care of the situation.

After all we had gone through I just couldn't believe at first what happened at new year. We had driven to work in our loyal yellow vehicle as usual, but when we tried to drive from work to the coast to spend the new year there, the van didn't start at all; it didn't even try. That probably doesn't sound so strange, but for us it was a total surprise and way too absurd to be true. Although we had had to make some repairs to the van, it had never left us on the road without warning. I trusted it and I felt that it trusted us. Our boss tried to find out what was wrong, but as he couldn't find anything obvious he towed us to a garage. The garage was just closing, so we didn't have any choice but to leave our home there and head back to the camping area. Our new year plans were ruined and we had to stay where we were.

We had taken the tent and some other little things we needed from the van. As I was sitting in front of the tent trying to figure out why this surprising situation had happened, I realized that I had never before believed in fate but that now my opinion was changing. The situation was way too weird to be a mere coincidence. It's still impossible for me to describe why it was so crucial to me that the van broke down at that particular moment. That the whole situation, and particularly the timing, was a coincidence wasn't simply enough for me. The weird restlessness – that for many days had been smoldering in the background – started to grow stronger and stronger. I couldn't even concentrate on celebrating new year with Jani and the other people in the camping area. All of a sudden, I was sure that I was supposed to be right there in Manjimup – I just didn't know why. I observed everything around me and waited to see what would happen next. Certainly something was happening or going to happen; I just didn't know what. The breaking down of the van had something to do with it. I tried to explain to Jani how I felt, and he too thought that the situation was surprising but not exceptional. Jani tried to calm me down and encourage me to celebrate the coming new year with the others. But it was no use and in the end I just wanted to sit in the tent by myself.

In spite of my expectations, nothing out of the ordinary happened during the next few days. Our yellow vehicle was parked in the garage waiting to be examined and everyday life went on without it. Our boss was very helpful and lent us a car to get to work and do our shopping. After new year our job changed and we started to gather and pack avocados instead of thinning the apple trees. It was a nice change. I had seen the man only in passing a couple of times but he was always in the company of another person. So I didn't talk with him about anything in particular.

A few days went by before I woke up very early one morning, around four o'clock. I had always been a sound sleeper, so waking up that early was very unusual for me. I felt very tired but at the same time wide awake. I lay quiet in the tent until the alarm clock went off and it was time to go to work. The weird restlessness felt really intense. It was very difficult for me to concentrate on work that day. I just kept sighing and my thoughts were bouncing here and there. I felt again a need to discuss our future with Jani. The moment was getting near when we would return to Finland, and I wanted to know what we would be doing in a couple of months. Jani shook his head. He didn't know what we should do either. We continued to gather the avocados. Soon I sighed deeply again and Jani heard.

– Should we break up then? he asked out of the blue.

– What?!

– Should we break up then? If neither of us knows what we want to do, perhaps we should consider breaking up. Jani is a very practical person and the suggestion was characteristic of him and his attitude towards life. He wanted to introduce an alternative we hadn't considered together yet.

– A-are you suggesting breaking up? I stammered looking at him in wonder. We had never before discussed breaking up.

– Let's give it a thought at leisure. I don't mean that we should necessarily separate. I just feel it'd be good to consider it. If we don't know what to do together, to be apart might be an alternative worth considering.

I was flabbergasted, and didn't know what to think. We had been together for almost six years, six wonderful years. He was the man I loved and with whom I had planned to spend the rest of my life. He was supposed to become my husband and the father of my children some day. It had never even occurred to me that we could separate. I thought our relationship was very good – intimate and balanced. Jani was just the man for me. We had had so many wonderful experiences together. At that very moment I was making my dream come true with him.

At first I thought I'd just ignore the proposition. I didn't even want to think about it. But the thought kept spinning in my mind. Soon I consciously imagined what the separation would feel like. I put the thought on the table right in front of me. At first I felt very sad and tears started running down my cheeks. I didn't want to be apart from Jani! I loved him! I didn't want to be alone. I didn't want to live without him. Soon the image grew bigger and bigger and began to frighten me. I can't even live without Jani! I simply can't live alone. I just can't! Then I would have nothing. Nothing at all! I would be nothing without him. Desperation overcame me and the whole idea began to feel unbearable. I felt how the fear inside me was growing. My heart was pounding, my body was trembling and I felt the need to throw up. Soon sheer terror overwhelmed me. I felt I was going to die. It was a truly horrible feeling. For a moment, I could neither breathe nor move. Everything stopped, literally everything.

As the terror reached a climax, everything changed all of sudden. The tower I had built came tumbling down. As if I had given up a heavy burden. As if somebody had emptied a balloon – and the balloon was myself. I was completely empty. I felt light and peaceful. I wanted to fly. I felt I was totally free. The tears of sorrow changed into the tears of joy. The feeling didn't last long but by being able to face my fear I had had an opportunity to have a glance behind my shell. I didn't then quite understand how important that experience was for me. I had looked the fear I had myself developed straight in the eye and therefore the self had been forced to loosen its grip. Nothing but nothing that comes from the self can tolerate the Presence of Love.

19

Love is not a need

Jani and I didn't discuss the possible separation any further. It was just one alternative among others, and our return to Finland was quite far off at the time. The situation forced me to concentrate even more tightly on the present moment: I understood that worrying about the future was of no use at that moment. Sometimes you just need to let things be. Neither of us had ever wanted to have any extra drama in our lives, not in our relationship or in anything else. That was one reason why we just let the matter rest. The self used other means in us to survive.

The strange restlessness in me continued and began to have a stronger effect on my nights. I slept badly and dreamt a lot. I woke up nearly every morning before the alarm clock went off, sometimes even two or three hours too early. I felt I was tired, but still fully awake. Somehow I was internally chaotic, yet externally there were no signs of it. As a matter of fact, I was very calm and quietly collected on the outside. I kept observing everything from aside. Maybe that was why I noticed the disgusting feeling inside me. It held me tightly in its grip. It was always there, sometimes on the surface, sometimes in the background.

One day after work I decided to walk back to the camping area. I wanted to be left in peace and enjoy a few kilometres walk. I had

had no chance to have any proper exercise for a long time and I noticed I was missing this familiar way of relaxing. Well, it wasn't always so relaxing but at least it usually calmed down my mind's spinning thoughts, at least for a moment. The road from our workplace to the camping area led through beautiful countryside. I hadn't been walking long before I noticed a familiar figure sitting in the field beside an old barn.

– What a coincidence! I said, half joking and half in earnest.

– Nice to see you, the man answered with a broad smile.

– It sure is. What are you doing here?

– Just hanging around, I mean my role character is.

– Do you want to be left alone? I've noticed that lots of people have visited your tent lately. Am I disturbing you?

– Not at all, just sit here beside me, the man said.

I did as the man suggested.

– You've got a lot of friends. So many people come to meet you, I said just to get the conversation going.

– Yes, it seems that word has got around. Many people want to know.

– Ah! Do you talk about life with them too? For some reason I was a little surprised.

– Yes, I talk about everything that Is.

I let my eyes rest on the peaceful countryside scenery for a while.

– Our van broke down, I said finally, breaking the silence around us.

– Oh.

– We've not yet been able to find out what's wrong with it. The garage promised to get in touch with us this week. It just broke down all of a sudden, and at new year on top of everything. We had a plan to sell it.

The man didn't comment on the news in any way, so we both sat there without saying a word, like so many times before. I pondered how to open the conversation in the best way.

– I still feel really restless. I don't even sleep well anymore. I don't believe that the van broke down by chance. Something's going on but I just don't know what. It's as if I was supposed to be right here, right now and nowhere else. As if it is really meant to be. As if this was the place where my whole life had led me, to Manjimup. All my choices have led me here, everything. Just as if it had been obvious that it's here that I will end up anyway. As if everything was predestined. A funny feeling, see?

The man nodded.

– I have never believed in any kind of destiny, but the time here in Manjimup has been somehow… I don't even know how to put it. Weird maybe? Too many coincidences. At first we didn't even mean to come here. We had never even heard of Manjimup. We just somehow drifted here.

– Yes, I see, the man said understandingly. – Just let things run their course. Trust Life. Like you said yourself, all kinds of weird – and inevitably scary – things will happen. But just trust Life. The inner Voice will help you.

I could have been frightened by his words but he looked so calm and certain. I trusted him. I trusted him but I wasn't yet able to fully trust Life in general.

– I'm trying, but it's not always easy.

– I understand that very well.

– By the way, I know now what everybody is looking for. Do you remember asking me?

– Sure I do.

– Everybody is looking for love. Everybody needs love. Without love there's nothing in life.

– What do you mean?

– Everybody wants love, even if they don't admit it, I repeated enthusiastically.

– And, why do you want love?

– Well… I can't live without love.

– That's true – you can't Live without Love. Why do you want it then?

I didn't understand what he was getting at.

– Well, everybody needs love. Because of the lack of love the whole situation on this planet is what it is. It's in a bad state because of the lack of love. Everybody shows symptoms because they don't feel love.

– You are right – everybody is looking for Love. Everybody wants Love. Everybody wants to find the way back. Nobody wants to walk in the labyrinth forever. However, you can never be lacking Love – it's completely impossible. Love Is, always. So the self is looking for something that you already Have, something that you Are.

– Just a minute. I didn't quite get it.

– You are looking for something that you already Have. The self needs something to be able to be something. For that reason you think you need love. But you can't need anything that you already Have.

– But I can't live without Jani, I retorted, revealing at the same time where the shoe really pinched. In this way I also revealed unintentionally how little I understood about Love.

– It means that the self can't live without a certain object.

– But I love Jani.

– You don't know what Love Is, the man said without a shade of doubt in his voice. – The self doesn't know what Love Is.

– Yes, I do know. I'm ready to die for Jani if it comes to that. The tone of my voice rose, because I felt hurt.

– Exactly. The self is ready to do anything not to lose its own existence. You don't need love but the self needs an object to be something. The self makes you believe that love is a need. But you can never really lose Love. Never – it's totally impossible.

– But maybe Jani doesn't want to be with me any more. I love him. I can't live without him, I almost sobbed and my eyes began to fill with tears.

The man remained sympathetically quiet and looked at me gently. When I finally was able to stop crying he continued.

– What in you can't live without Jani?

– Well, I. I can't live without Jani. I don't understand the question. I looked at the man in astonishment. I hadn't really listened to what he had just explained. I was so entangled in my own idea about love.

– The self wants to imprison love in a cage and then introduce it to others. The self needs, it doesn't Love.

– I don't want to put Jani in any kind of cage.

– The self wants to own the object it needs, it wants to own love. The self doesn't want anybody to be free. It makes the object it needs "mine". The self makes that object a part of itself. The self needs something to be something. Love doesn't need. Love Is.

– I will certainly lose a big part of love if I lose Jani.

– You will just lose something you think you need. What does Jani give you?

I was lost for words again and just looked at the man in wonder.

– The self builds and maintains relationships – any kind of relationship – solely because it needs something. When this something is a human relationship the self makes you believe that you need this relationship. In other words, you feel that you are lacking something, so by maintaining the relationship you try – and manage temporarily – to get something that covers this feeling of lack. As I mentioned before, every need originates in the feeling of lack. What will you be lacking if there is no Jani any more?

– What! Jani, of course!

– Jani is nothing other than a bunch of thoughts. Jani is a story composed of memories. Jani is a role character you have developed yourself, a character your self needs and with whom you want to perform on the stage. He is just a role character whose thoughts and body you need – a role character who is just a thought, a thought which has acquired a shape.

– So? A role character or not. I love Jani. I love Jani's role character, I said, feeling very hurt because the man just didn't comprehend how much I loved my companion.

– You said that you can't live without Jani, the man continued with calm determination. – Well, it may be true. The more you need something, the tighter you identify yourself with it. The more an object gives you, the tighter you cling to it. The self does everything in its power to preserve its existence. The self needs different kinds of objects. It needs something to be able to be something, the man kept repeating. – The self makes you believe that you won't be able to manage or even live without an object, and therefore makes you dependent on it. Any object will do as long as the self can make you feel you need it.

I began to calm down because I gradually began to comprehend that the man really didn't want to hurt me at all. I had, of course, been aware of that before, but couldn't help my natural reaction.

– Well, we already discussed feelings, and how the self clings to different feelings. A certain object seems to create a feeling or feelings that you don't want to let go. The feeling may be a physical or a mental dependence. Different dependences are often interconnected. In other words, Jani gives you feelings that you need. You have built an entity which is composed of different feelings and on which you are dependent. This dependence isn't always connected with a human being. It may just as well be directed to tobacco, alcohol, medicines, drugs or certain food. One can just as well experience dependence for a certain object or residence, job, hobby, skill, status, or pet, for example. The object that you feel you love most, that you feel you need most is the object that gives you most.

I began to feel a great need to defend my dependency. I felt threatened.

– But an alcoholic doesn't love alcohol. Alcoholism is a disease. I don't think needing a drink is quite the same thing as needing a person.

– An alcoholic needs alcohol, and according to your concept, loves it. After all, it doesn't matter what the object is – it is your self that gives it the meaning you want. For some people, alcohol can mean more than any person. They need alcohol more than they need someone. The need is the same, but the object different. It makes no difference what the object is; the most important thing is the feeling it produces, which gives something to the experiencer. As I've already mentioned, the feeling can be either pleasant or unpleasant; the self doesn't care. It only wants to generate a feeling it can identify itself with.

The man's outspoken words aroused a need in me to defend myself, although at the same time I understood that there was no need for that. So I decided not to say anything.

– For you one of the objects is obviously Jani, the man continued.
– Jani gives you something you need physically and mentally. Am I right?

– I guess, I admitted reluctantly. I had just admitted my dependency on Jani, which produced conflicting feelings in me. On the one hand, I was irritated and distressed but, on the other, I felt relieved in a strange way.

– You feel you are part of Jani. You are part of everything that is connected with you and Jani. You are part of your relationship, a thought which you have named love. You have developed this thought, and with its help, a bunch of feelings you need.

The strange feeling of relief vanished as fast as it had appeared, and anxiety and growing irritation was all that was left. The man began to get on my nerves more and more. Did he even do it on purpose? Gritting my teeth, I sat, however, completely still and quiet.

– The self clings to everything it identifies itself with. You don't need Jani, or any other specific object, to be able to Love. You can just Love.

My irritation, my slight feeling of hatred, began to turn into sadness again.

– But I will be sad without Jani.

– Do you see now how the self acts? First the idea of love feels good and the next moment it feels bad. The passion turns from sorrow into hatred. Real Love is not a bunch of different feelings – and particularly not a feeling producing suffering. What part in you becomes sad? What part in you wants to shut love in a cage? What part in you doesn't want to let Jani go free?

I supposed that the man didn't even expect me to answer these questions, so I remained quiet.

– Love doesn't need anything. Love is not dependent on an object or any feeling derived from it. Love only gives. Love only Loves. The self needs. The self doesn't know what Love Is. The self has only created a thought of love. But Love is not a thought. Love is nothing you believe it is. Love is not an idea you've made up yourself.

– You can't possibly suggest that I don't love Jani, genuinely love! It felt impossible to let go.

– I don't want to suggest anything. Of course, You can Love. What you Are does nothing but Love. It is only your self that is incapable of

Love. Your self only needs the thought of love, the thought you have made up, the thought that gives something to your self. I don't mean to hurt you, I just want to help you discover something very import-ant. Observe what part in you needs Jani and is afraid of losing him. The self preserves its existence making use of need and fear. You can never suffer because of Love – only the thought of love creates suffering. Neither can you ever be afraid because of Love – only the thought of love can scare you.

– Your words sound so strange. To my mind – and I think most people think in the same way – it is love that may cause the most suffering and fear. I don't think I'm the only one who needs loved ones – or love in general.

– Love never causes suffering or fear, it is your self that causes these feelings. Suffering and fear can't, in fact, even be separated from each other because suffering always originates in fear. But let's not get stuck with names. The main thing is that you are aware of the fact that suffering and fear have nothing to do with Love. It is worth trying to observe what in you produces suffering. The same source fears and causes suffering as a result.

– You are speaking as if there was another kind of love than the one I know.

– There is no other kind of love. There is nothing but Love. You have only developed your own idea of love – you only have your own beliefs as to what love is.

– Are you saying that I don't know what love is? I was getting an-noyed again.

– What you See in Jani is in everything else too. Look around. It is not separate from anything. Something just prevents you from See-ing It. You can't lose It; you can only lose the thought of It.

I looked around. What was the "it" the man was talking about?

– Nobody can love everybody and everything, I said.

– No, no one can. The shell only sees the shell.

– I just can't get the hang of it, I said shaking my head.

– It is impossible to describe in words what Is. Just go on observ-ing yourself neutrally. Pay attention to all your thoughts about Jani in particular. What in you wants to cling and fear? What in you needs? What is it in you that suffers? You are not the source of all that. That source is an illusion that only wants to keep its own existence.

I felt ill at ease and anxious. I felt threatened once more.

– I don't know… I think I have to continue my walk to the camping area. Our conversation is of no help to me right now. My mind has gone haywire – and now all this talk of love on top of it; I just don't understand anything. I need time to think about all this.

– That's right. Nevertheless, it's good for you to know that what you are looking for is not separate from anything. It is everywhere and in everything. It has always been and will always be. It cannot be gained or lost – It just Is. You just have to find the source in yourself that prevents you from knowing It, the source that stops you from Seeing.

– I really don't know what to think of all of this. Let's continue our talk some other time, okay? My restless was growing stronger and stronger, and I wanted to end the conversation. I wanted to go away. I wanted to escape. I wanted to run away, far from all this.

– Suits me fine, the man said smiling his irresistible smile.

Me, I didn't feel like smiling at all, so I just got up and started walking towards the camping area.

20

Love Is

At that time I didn't understand yet what the man meant by Love. I didn't understand that not even the word Love (or any other word) could really describe Love. I felt hurt and irritated because the idea of love meant a lot to me. In the end, it meant so much to me that it crushed me. The shell that my own idea of love had held together broke and set me free for real Love, which is something so indescribable that even an attempt to do so is like trying to describe the sun by examining only one of its rays. This Love Is something that you wouldn't believe can exist. After finding this Love the search is over, the labyrinth collapses and only everything that Is is left. In Manjimup I was still walking in the labyrinth. The walls had begun to shake but they were still standing. The Love that finally broke the labyrinth I had built myself – that pushed through my shell and rose up from under the frozen ground – is so strong and firm that simply nothing can stop It. Not one thought that causes suffering can even graze It. No fear can stop It from proceeding. Love is as hard as rock and at the same time as soft as cotton wool. It will stand forever and will not waver. It supports and extends.

The thought of love produces a whole lot of feelings. Everyone has ideas of their own about love. Some blush when thinking of love, some might nod their heads knowingly, some feel warmth in the heart and others great responsibility on their shoulders. One may get angry and the other may not even want to think of it. If Love had an opposite – which is impossible – it would be fear, for fear is the strongest defence force of the self. Making use of fear the self has created a whole lot of ideas of love.

One of the most influential ideas is god. The self has developed the idea of an almighty god who loves us on certain conditions. This example, which is based on if-love, is very common and has a great effect on the general idea we have about love. Nevertheless, Love is unconditional. Love doesn't accuse or judge; it is completely Free. For many people marriage is the symbol of love, but Love is no symbol and It is not binding. Love is not an obligation, sacrifice or a way to act. Love has no model of action, It Is Now. Neither is Love a relationship – human or any other – to which it is often connected.

Everybody knows what Love really Is. It is a sheer impossibility to even imagine otherwise. But the shell only sees the shell, and to be able to remember again what Love Is you have to see the shell first and then move it aside. I saw in Manjimup only a shell through my shell, but later this shell broke. For that reason I urge you to look around. What is left when you move all the roles aside? What is left when you take off the role costumes of your friends, parents, siblings, children, spouse, pets and colleagues, the costumes that you have sewn to them yourself? What is left when you put aside the identity of the person standing in front of you? What is left when there is nobody to love or hate any more? What is left when the person standing in front of you is not a woman or a man, a homosexual or a heterosexual, a boss or a president, a cleaning lady or a bus driver, an old person or a youth, a killer or a nun, a TV celebrity or a guru, a wise man or an idiot? What is left when the opinions and feelings of the person standing in front of you are moved aside? What is left when your opinions and feelings are moved aside? I urge you to look at yourself in the mirror. Look deep into your eyes. What is left when there is no body anymore? What is left when the person looking at the image in the mirror disappears? What is left when the story that is composed of memories is laid down like a sack that has been a burden on your shoulders? What is shining through the shell?

Love only Loves. That is why I urge you to observe what it is in you that hates and becomes distressed. What in you accuses and judges and doesn't forgive? What in you craves for revenge and attack? What compares, envies and becomes bitter? What clings, worries and fears? What in you is not able to Love, yourself or anyone else? What in you causes suffering and different kinds of illnesses? What in you is constantly restless and feels lack? What tries and tries and gets stressed? What part is dissatisfied and lies? What in you doesn't want you to enjoy and feel Joy? What in you doesn't want you to be Happy and Free? What part in you doesn't want you to do what you'd really like to do? What part makes you feel guilt and feels guilty? What part is intolerant and discriminative? What part doesn't want to understand? What in you doesn't trust? What part in you doesn't know what Love Is?

You have to be fed up of this source before you can continue your journey. You have to be so totally fed up of it that nothing else counts any more. You have to be sick of suffering. You have to be sick of your self.

In your heart of hearts you want to know what you really Are – either consciously or unconsciously. You have been looking and looking around you, searching every nook and corner, and every time you believe you have found what you were looking for, you cling to it tooth and nail. You feel restless and don't know where to look any more. Even if you don't see in front of you anything other than the road of despair, you don't stop to look directly inside you. You simply just don't realize to stop and check the most obvious place. You can't believe that after all this searching – which may have continued on a conscious level for years – you already Have what you are looking for. You cannot possibly believe that after all the clinging, you have all the time Had what you have been afraid to lose. You don't need anything to be able to find. You don't need anything to be able to know.

21

The self is afraid of what you Are

During the next few days the strange restlessness in me was nearly intolerable. I began to feel that the environment was cheating me in some way, as if I was playing cops and robbers. I was the cop and the robbers were hiding somewhere near me. Every time I felt a hunch and glanced in that direction, there was nothing to be seen. Still, I felt that the robbers were jeering at me from somewhere very near. Well, I had just been too slow once again. Being slow somehow describes my condition at the time. I knew instinctively that something was happening around me but every time I stopped to think about it everything was as it had always been. I couldn't keep up the pace, or maybe it was the environment that couldn't keep up with me. I felt like Jim Carrey in the movie *The Truman Show.*

The fear inside me grew stronger. I began to analyse my own conduct and the churning strange feeling inside me. I began to doubt the man's intentions. Had I been mixed up in something suspicious? There were moments I even doubted my own sanity. I felt really restless and soon didn't dare to go to the toilet in the camping area alone at night. I observed everything and waited on what would happen next. Naturally Jani wondered why I was behaving like that. He thought that I was frighteningly absent at times, although I didn't tell him anything of the state I was in. It had been me and me alone who had joined in the man's "game". I felt I was responsible for the situation. Externally I was still calm, continuing our everyday work in Manjimup in the normal way. I tried to calm myself down and decided not to see the man any more. Everything would certainly come back to normal if I let some time go by. To me, back to normal meant to the the time before the strange restlessness began.

Nothing, however, went back to normal. In fact, more strange things were happening to me. A change in my menstrual cycle was one of them. It had always been very regular, but now the cycle started again after only two weeks. I could have understood why my period was late but too early was something that baffled me. I actually doubted whether it was biologically possible at all. My whole body went into overdrive. It was apparent that what was happening was happening both inside of me as well as outside; at that time I still saw myself as separate from the environment.

Nearly every morning, I woke before the alarm clock went off. In the evenings I fell asleep almost instantly because I was really exhausted after the day. I used all my energy to hold myself together. Work and everyday chores in general seemed to make it a little easier to bear; I wanted to keep moving. If I stopped it seemed too much to tolerate. There were moments when I felt I was at the end of my tether. I was afraid I would break down. I was tired but wide awake. I had no appetite but I forced myself to eat something just to keep Jani from worrying. He had wondered before what had suddenly happened to me, but now my weird behaviour had continued for far too long. Having Jani worrying about me was the last thing I wanted, so I did my best to behave normally. Jani tried to ask me what it was all about. I answered that I just had a lot to think about – and sure enough that was true! I tried to understand and analyze what was going on. I was scared and didn't know what to do. I knew that neither Jani nor anybody else could help me, and I didn't want to see the man any more. Thinking about it afterwards I wonder how I was able to behave almost normally in the midst of all those waves of turmoil and fear. Apart from Jani nobody else noticed anything strange in my behaviour. I didn't know at the time that I was supported by Something that can never fail. It was the foundation on which I had built my life – and at the same time my reality – that was failing.

Time went on until one day I was sure that there was more to life than what could be experienced through the senses. I had suspected it before but now I knew. Cold shivers trickled through my body. For some time I tried to make myself believe otherwise. It is incredible how the self tried to deny the truth until the end, even when I was sure of it. A source I didn't know had cheated me and was still trying to cheat me and all the others. I had now found this out. I knew something the others didn't know, something I couldn't explain, something I couldn't even understand myself. That something was Something. I was more alert than before, if that was in any way possible. For some time now I had behaved more like a timid deer than what I thought of as my balanced self. All the people close to me considered me a very balanced person, but now the balanced foundation on which my whole identity rested started to be quite shaky.

I changed my mind and decided to go and see the man. He was the only one I could talk to. I had mixed feelings about this. On the one hand, the man had been right, but on the other hand, I felt I had gotten mixed up in something that I shouldn't have had any idea about. I still didn't know what that something was. All I knew now was that The Something Was.

It didn't take long before I found myself in front of the small green tent calling the man. Soon he put his head out of the tent.

– Oh, hello, Sanna.

I skipped the usual greetings and went straight to business.

– I know. I admit this isn't it. You were right. I just came to ask you what it is that I know. I mean that I'm certain about Something but I just don't know what It is. I'm sure you can reveal that to me now.

I looked at him, waiting to be answered. He came out of the tent.

– There's nothing to say.

My patience - which had already been tried severely - began to reach its breaking point.

– Don't start again! I know that you know. It was because of you that all this started anyway. Now I know too, thanks to you, I guess. Isn't it only fair that you tell me what this is all about?

The man looked at me for a while and obviously noticed I was serious and that now was no time for joking.

– Let's sit down and talk in peace.

– I'm not sitting down anywhere. I've had enough of our little talks. I just want to know what's going on. The tone of my voice was very tight. I can honestly say I hadn't blown my fuse many times in adulthood and normally I was surprisingly patient. Of course it's true I had been on edge earlier too because of the man and the things he'd been telling me, but I had somehow always managed to keep the situation together. Now I was almost a mental wreck and my self control began to fail.

– Can you explain a bit closer what you mean? The man asked calmly, irritatingly calmly.

– No one will cheat me anymore, not you or anybody else. Something smells fishy. I know that now for certain. Tell me what it is!

– Just sit down, and I'll tell you, he said and looked straight into my eyes.

I sighed deeply again and sat down beside him.

– You are going through a process.

– WHAT?!?

– You are going through a process.

– WHAT FUCKING PROCESS? I never used bad language – never – but now I had reached the limit.

The man didn't say anything, just looked at me calmly. Suddenly I felt cold shivers running down my spine. Now I knew! Help! Now I knew!

– Is Matrix true? I asked flabbergasted.

– What Matrix are you talking about? The man answered.

– The movie! I'll be damned! Matrix is real! I've always thought that it's only a movie. Why didn't I come to think of it earlier? I was shaking my head in disbelief.

The man didn't say anything.

– And now I know! I felt myself going slowly into a panic. – You're one of them, aren't you? Is somebody coming to get me now? Are you taking me away to some space ship now?!

– Calm down. Nobody is taking you anywhere, the man answered calmly, too calmly I thought.

– Don't lie to me! Tell me the truth! I know that life isn't what people think it is. I know it. I don't want to go any further. I've changed my mind. I don't want to know! I'm not going anywhere! I don't want to swallow a red pill! I begged, aware that I was gradually being overwhelmed by fear.

– What on earth are you talking about? The man looked at me questioningly.

Right then I understood – help! – I had already chosen the red pill! When I made the conscious decision to find out, I had already made my choice. There was no way I could go back now.

– Sanna, listen to me a moment. Nobody is taking you anywhere. You have just developed a fear for yourself. The self does anything to preserve its existence.

– But I know! Why is something kept secret? Nobody has the slightest idea. I know something. I know It intuitively.

– I believe you. Just trust your Intuition. You'll soon feel better.

After a while I was able to pull myself together again, at least to the extent that in spite of being afraid, I was able to form some kind of clear idea in my head.

– Are you talking about the strange feeling? I can't trust that. I'm literally coming apart if I let it take over. There's no way I can hold myself together. You can't understand what the last few days have been like. I don't know how long I will be able to take it anymore. I'm mentally and physically completely exhausted. I haven't been myself for several weeks.

– I understand what you mean all right. Surely this time is very confusing and scary for you. But you will be quite all right. The strange feeling isn't your enemy. It is your self who is trying to make it an enemy; the self takes advantage of the fear. In fact, the strange feeling is your Friend – your dearest Friend. Just trust It.

– So, you do know what I mean? And there's nobody coming to get me for sure? I haven't even had the courage to go to the toilet during the night.

– You can be sure that nobody is taking you anywhere. You have just created the fear for yourself.

– This is quite mad – I don't have a clue what this is all about. Some Power rules here – or it's not a power at all. I can't even explain what I mean.

– I know very well what you mean. Now you just have to try to rest. There's nothing to worry about.

– So you don't know either what It is!?

The man didn't say anything. I understood later that he couldn't have said anything because then I would have clung to the thought I had created. I wasn't able to connect the feeling with Love yet because I was too scared of It myself.

– I don't know what to do. I'm scared, I said in a shaky voice.

– You can stay here and rest if you like. I don't think it's of any use to talk any more. You really need to rest, but I promise there's nothing for you to worry about.

I trusted the man. Although I had tried to tell myself something else, inside I had actually trusted him all along.

– All right, I believe you. I'll go and have a rest. Jani is reading a book in the tent, I'll go to him.

– Good idea. If you need me I'll be here too.

– Thank you. I'm sorry I lost it again. I just had to talk to someone. Jani can't understand me – nor can anyone else.

– I know that. You can always come to me when you feel like it.

– Thank you, I said relieved, and hugged the man.

– I want you to know one more thing. The truth Is beautiful, incredibly beautiful. Your self is just scared of It, the man called out to me as I started out towards our tent.

22

Acceptance

The following night I slept like a log, soundly and contentedly. The nights after that were restless again, but I still felt better after one peaceful night. I understood that something was happening and that everything wasn't as I had always supposed. But I couldn't do anything about it. For one reason or another, I just had to go through everything that was happening. For some reason I knew Something but I didn't understand It. I felt uncomfortable but could do nothing about it. It was best for me to just accept the situation and trust Life. I surrendered to Life. Giving in doesn't feel the right expression because I didn't feel I was giving in. I just accepted because I simply realized that resistance was quite futile. What I knew Was, whether I wanted It or not. I could do nothing about It. I sensed Its immovable, unyielding Existence. I still didn't want to think about It. I didn't want to face It. I just let It be.

Gradually, I began to feel better. I didn't observe everything as fanatically as I had done previously. I was still anxious and couldn't trust the environment completely. I was alert but the fervent fear began to loosen its grip on me. I didn't frantically rush from one thing to another anymore but observed calmly what was happening around me. I began to pay attention to things I hadn't even noticed before – Life began to show me a new side of Itself. I could follow a flying butterfly or fluttering tree leaves for a long time. Everything seemed to be fully alive and somehow very lively and beautiful. I wondered why I had never noticed that before.

More surprising things started to happen, but this time they brought me Joy and genuine wonder at life's remarkableness. I finally realized that I didn't understand anything about life. I began to sense more and more strongly that I had to let everything be just as it was and accept everything as it is. This new perception gave rise to the understanding that later on crystallized into a perfect truth, the truth according to which everything Is as it Is. I wasn't aware then how important this acceptance was; without acceptance you cannot find the way to the Destination. By accepting – not by submitting – I took a big step towards the Freedom I could have never even dreamt of.

After this I met the man a couple of more times in passing. We didn't talk long. I felt he had nothing to say to me anymore. As if I already knew everything I was supposed to know. The man simply urged me to be patient and trust Life. I told him about my new discoveries, and he only said smiling that Life was full of surprises. He also said that if I kept an open mind and was ready to receive, Life would show me everything. This thought was a little frightening to me because I could not yet fully trust what was to come.

Jani noticed I had calmed down, but still the worry didn't leave him. He wondered why I just stared at the grass and everything else around me. He couldn't understand why I was suddenly so interested in the greenness of the bushes or the gentleness of the wind in my hair. He thought my behaviour was weird, to say the least. I was too calm and serene, and didn't behave normally at all. I could very well understand why he thought so. For the last few months, or actually the last few years, I had made him run from one place or event to another. My need "to live life to the full" had reached a culmination when we were realizing our dream. During the journey I had wanted to see and experience everything, just everything, more and more all the time, and still nothing seemed to suffice. There was always something new and interesting on offer. I planned our daily program so that we could get the most out of it. We tried everything new, from diving to parachute jumping, saw an incredible number of fascinating places, met different kinds of people and admired exotic animals. Nothing, however, seemed to be enough for me. I wanted more, endlessly more. The earth was like Aladdin's cave to me and I wanted to see and experience everything on it. And now, all of a sudden, I was content with a stalk of grass swaying in front of me. If I'd been Jani I would certainly have been worried as well. I calmed him down and said that I was just tired, although I also urged him to look at everything too and really see what there was around him.

The days went by and our time in Manjimup was coming to an end. Although the time had passed quickly everything still happened like a slow-motion movie. In a week we were supposed to continue our journey to Perth. The van had been towed to a scrap yard the week before. When the garage told us they were not able to find what was wrong with it we had taken it to another garage. When the other garage couldn't find the problem either (very odd!) we decided to give up our dear van. We had no time or energy to examine further what had caused the surprising break down of the van. I told Jani that whatever the reason it was meant to be. Our yellow home had done its job and taken care of us as long as it was meant to do so. My understanding of life had increased. I had accepted the fact that I couldn't control everything. I had a hunch that it was better for me to just step aside and let Life take over. I was on the way towards perfect trust that later became so strong and lasting that nothing or nobody could even try to shake It. I wasn't really fully There yet but my journey towards the freeing trust had clearly begun.

The last week in Manjimup went by very fast. On the day before our departure we said goodbye to our boss and his family, and all our other new friends in the camping area. I went to see the man once more. I thanked him for everything with tears in my eyes. I felt restless again because soon I would be alone. Soon I would have nobody near me to help me when I was in distress. By distress I meant the fear that still kept whispering into my ear. I had not wanted to think about the strange feeling, and by ignoring It I had managed to built some kind of balance to lean on. The balance I had built myself was not, however, permanent. It only gave me temporary relief behind which I wanted to hide. The man assured me once more that everything was alright. I just had to trust and let Life lead me. He asked me to confide solely in my inner Voice. He also handed me a piece of paper on which was written vipassana and the name of a book that he said was worth buying. I had never heard about the book, neither did I know what "vipassana" meant. I hugged the man and thanked him from the bottom of my heart. I felt really sad but I also knew that once more I just had to accept things as they were. It was time for me to continue my journey instead of clinging to what I thought I needed. I now trusted Life more than the fear that was following me.

As I have already mentioned, acceptance is of utmost importance. Without acceptance it is not possible to know what really Is. Each of us has his or her own unique path to tread. No matter what your path is like, no matter how difficult and unjust it seems to be, it is the very path that you should walk. When you get to the destination you will know why. You will understand why your path was just what it had to be.

23

The bubble bursts

The restlessness didn't leave me but it didn't overwhelm me entirely either. After arriving in Perth I was glad we had left Manjimup. The change of place did me good because the time in Manjimup had been very intense and frantic – I can't really describe it any other way. Much more had happened in those couple of months than I was able to digest. Now I felt the need to just be. I didn't want to contemplate anything, I just wanted to live one day at a time.

I had not been in touch with anybody in Finland after new year, and I knew that many people from home were wondering what had happened. I didn't know what to write to them. Something had happened and was still happening to me, Something I couldn't even explain to myself. I had always been very honest and that is why I wanted to try somehow to tell the others what was happening to me. I knew that it was soon time to return to Finland, and for some reason that thought didn't cause any stress for me anymore. Actually my excitement started to grow because soon I could see my family and friends again. I arranged a meeting in June, and promised to tell everybody what had happened. I hadn't the slightest idea of what I was going to say but I trusted that everything would become clear to me. Life in general was quite confusing to me at the time, and I didn't know what exactly was going on.

After Perth we flew to Adelaide where we rented a new van. We wanted to cruise around and admire the scenery all the way to Melbourne. After two days' driving we got a couple of worried phone calls from Finland. On the drive we had, in fact, been surprised to learn that we weren't allowed near an inland camping area. But we soon got to know why. There was a shockingly large bush fire in the inland area, and news about it had even reached Finnish television. The fire had spread – and was still spreading – incredibly fast. People had difficulties getting out of its way even in cars. We calmed down our loved ones and told them that we were quite alright. We were on the coast and the fire was at least two hundred kilometers away inland.

I hadn't read anything for months but after Manjimup I decided I would take reading up again. Generally when we stopped in a camping area, I willingly grabbed a book because I felt I could concentrate on reading again. The book I was reading was a novel, in English, and based on true events. We had been given it as a Christmas present. I hadn't yet gotten hold of the book the man had recommended. I had only read one book in English, and it hadn't been an easy job for me because I really don't have a head for languages, although I have travelled quite a lot and often spoken English. Or rather tried to speak - I mumbled, stammered and explained, but at least I tried! The conversation with the man had gone amazingly well, and with the help of a dictionary you can manage surprising well with many challenges.

The three weeks after leaving Manjimup flew past quickly. I still wasn't quite as restless as in Manjimup but I wasn't calm either. Life wasn't the same as it had been a couple of months earlier. I was more sensitive to what was happening around me, and there were many interesting coincidences. My trust in Life became deeper, I slept better and had a stronger appetite. I felt rested. Looking back at the situation now I could say that Life allowed me a moment's rest, and that's exactly what it felt like because soon my mind was in turmoil again – and this time it was even stronger. The feeling I had tried to ignore kept growing until it was so strong that I had no other alternative than to face It. But this encounter was still a way off because I wasn't ready for it just yet.

Something happened in Melbourne that brought everything to the surface again, something so harmless that I couldn't have guessed it would be so influential: I read the book the man had recommended. I bought it in a bookstore and even though I read the back cover, I didn't quite understand what it was about. Many people would probably describe it as a spiritual book.

I knew intuitively that I should read the book. When I had finished the novel, I decided with a strong determination that I would get through it, even with my bad english. Luckily I did so because later I understood that the words in the book were not the point, rather the insights that bubbled up from deep within. I was reading the book in the hostel and, all of a sudden, I just knew! I knew what the man had tried to explain to me all the time: I'm not me! I'm not myself! Incredible!!! As if I had woken up from some kind of dream. I sat for a moment on the edge of my bed, my mouth open, and then burst into a crazy laughter of relief. Jani was looking at me with eyes like saucers because he didn't have a clue what was going on.

– I'm not me, I'm not really Sanna! I'm not my mind nor my body, I kept repeating over and over.

The next day we went into downtown Melbourne, but instead of admiring all the usual sights I kept staring around me. People were like robots. As if I was watching a movie. As if I had woken up from a dream which others were still clearly dreaming. I felt like yelling at the top of my voice: "WAKE UP! Everything is just a dream, every-thing!" I didn't, however, start shouting wake-up calls right there and then. What would people have thought? Probably they would have just stared at me for a long while and then shaken their heads. But I still wanted to shout like crazy and if I had done so I would have been like all those people who walk the streets mumbling to themselves or on the soapbox preaching to others.

Suddenly a new fear raised its head: I can't talk about this, I can't say anything about this to anybody. People will think I'm mad if I start talking about what has happened to me. You can't explain it even to yourself, let alone to anybody else. HELP! If I talked about this to somebody I would probably be taken away somewhere out of sight. There would be official-looking white-coated men who would take me away in a white car to a place from which I could never get away. I would have to explain my behaviour and promise that I would never again be red faced, shouting wake-up calls in the middle of the street because it is by no means a decent thing to do and people would be disturbed and I would be breaking the order of things. And the rules; they have to be observed at any cost! Everything must go on unchanged. It doesn't matter to where or why, it has to go on just as before! A white-coated man tries to calm me down looking very serious. I apologise for my behaviour once more and explain that I'm only a foolish tourist from Finland, and that's what we do in Finland, and I do understand very well that my behaviour is completely thoughtless and not appropriate here in Australia. I promise – really promise – not to say another word. I will be quiet from now on. Let people just live their lives. Let them run in the circles they have created. Let them wander aimlessly. Let them go on searching. The nurses are just shaking their heads, looking at me with great pity. I ask to get back to my companion because naturally they haven't allowed Jani to come with me in the car because it's just for those who are mad. Nobody would listen to me or take me seriously anyway – why would they, since in their opinion I was mad.

Suddenly I find myself sitting at a table and opposite me sits an aged woman with an official smile. Her smile is not supposed to reveal, it is supposed to look genuine. I notice it anyway and smile back because I know what will happen next. I will be bombarded with questions. Feeling like a fool, I explain how I realized yesterday all of a sudden how life is only an act. People are sleepwalking and nobody's got a clue. When I was walking over there in the street this new revelation just felt like too big a lump to swallow, and that is why I started yelling. That's all. I just let some steam out. The woman is looking at me again, smiling officially and inviting me to continue. And of course, I explain and explain and explain until she doesn't need to hear anymore. I tell her that I have just started but at the same time I realize that I've already said way too much. Naturally she can't understand my words. Of course they sound quite insane to her. Help! Do I always have to be so honest? All explanations are, however, futile because the woman has already formed a picture of me: who could take a lunatic's words seriously? Help! The panic starts to spread. Everybody really thinks I've gone out of my mind. Soon I will be taken away. I'm afraid Jani will not come and fetch me because naturally he's been told that it's best for me to be here. Jani, of course, believes them since my conduct has been quite strange for a while already. I haven't been myself for a long time – there must be something wrong with me. Jani only wants what's best for me, and he's been told that this place is the best for me right now. My family will understand later too that it's better for Sanna to be in an asylum for a time. My friends will be sad for me too, for no one would wish for such a miserable ending to my journey of dreams. I'm trapped with other lunatics. I try to escape but I'm caught. My restless, downright aggressive behaviour isn't normal. The nurses decide to tie me up in my bed with leather straps and give me a couple of electric shocks, zapp zapp.

Just a minute! Wake up! Me myself! I stop playing with thoughts and walk along calmly beside Jani as if nothing had happened. Nobody can understand me anyway – they just can't. I decide to keep my mouth shut because nobody will know that I know if I keep quiet. I'd better just behave normally and act like one of the others.

I understood that what I had found out was something big, shockingly big, something I had had no idea of before. Well, I had had a hunch of something but I still could not imagine in my wildest dreams what I now knew. I wondered how many people knew? The man knew, that was clear. But who else? Should I inform someone? Was there some kind of a conspiracy in the world that knew about it? Or did somebody already know I knew? Would there be somebody coming to get me after all? Whatever the situation I understood that I couldn't do anything about it. I just had to accept that everything is as it is.

Although I understood I wasn't Sanna, the self slyly continued its manoeuvres. I knew now that I wasn't the actor on the stage but I identified myself with the person watching the performance. There was still something in me which felt it was here, alive, watching everything from aside. The self did everything to preserve its existence. The self had now been revealed to me and it tried to repair the web I had torn apart. The self tried to cover what I knew. It started to develop more fears to make the web whole again. But I had already seen too much; I knew what there was behind the web. I couldn't possibly deny it anymore.

This was followed by an extremely difficult period of time which could perhaps be described as a battle between my self and me. I wouldn't, however, call it a battle because the end result was decided in advance – I just didn't know it. Love doesn't fight. Love has no need to attack or defend. Love cannot feel Itself threatened. My self fought. It was myself fighting against My Self. My self fought against Something That I could never beat. Love didn't do anything. Love just Was and Is. Love just waited patiently until I lay my weapons down.

24

Death

The next day we left for Sydney on a bus. I felt really mixed up. Thoughts were bouncing here and there. I tried to calm down but occasionally it felt quite impossible. I decided to listen to music because I needed some way to calm myself. From the bottom of my heart I thanked the person who had invented the mp3-player.

In Sydney my condition was unchanged. I walked with Jani from one place to another trying to hold myself together. My feelings changed from one extreme to another. I could cry for Joy and feel indescribable Peace in the morning, and then be scared of almost anything during the daytime. The fears swept over me like waves. I felt restless but still trusting. The foundation built by the self had crashed down at last, and my life, my whole life and reality had rested on it. These were the first moments I was standing on new Ground. Of course, It had always been there, but I just hadn't been aware of It. I had always trusted the foundation I had built myself – as I didn't even know there was anything else. The self tried to build a new shaky foundation on the One I was consciously standing on now. It tried to make me believe in its strong existence, and partly I still listened to it. The voice of the self still sounded so very real because I had listened to it all my life. But the new Voice grew stronger and stronger every moment. It was certain and endlessly patient. I trusted It more and more every day. The Voice wasn't afraid, not even for a single moment. It didn't even know what fear was. It was my self that tried to fight against It. The self didn't understand – or didn't want to understand – that it didn't have any chance at all. The self couldn't possibly win since there was nothing to win. In Sydney I didn't understand yet that the self had developed this whole fight itself. That what Is just Was and It didn't have to do anything in order to Be.

I observed myself again like a hawk. I knew now what the source of my unpleasant feelings was but I still couldn't do anything about it. I watched Sanna performing her incoherent role on the stage. I was in the middle of a storm-cloud but couldn't chase it away. Sanna wanted to understand. Sanna wanted answers to questions she had herself formed. For Sanna, the Truth was too much. Sanna was scared. Sanna didn't understand. I knew that it was me myself that caused the suffering. I tried to concentrate on what I was doing in the moment, but my thoughts were bouncing around like lottery balls. The only thing I could do was to trust, just to trust one moment at a time. No thought producing suffering or a feeling reflected from it can last forever if you are ready to face it, to feel it in the present moment.

Jani was worried. He didn't know anymore what to do or say. He couldn't comprehend why I was behaving in the way I was. He was full of questions: What had happened? What was still happening? Why didn't I behave normally? Why wasn't I the familiar well-balanced Sanna? Why couldn't I leave everything alone? Why did I think that the book was so meaningful? Why had I started the conversations with the man in the first place? He had clearly mixed my head up. The book had mixed my head up. Why couldn't I just forget? Jani was really afraid. He was afraid for me and for himself. He didn't want to accuse me of anything – he just wanted to understand what was happening. He wanted to understand Something I couldn't even explain to myself. I told him that this was not all there is, everything wasn't as he thought it was. I invited him to read the book too, then he would understand but he refused even to touch it. If it was that book that had driven me crazy he didn't want to have anything to do with it. He was referring to my changing moods. I tried to soothe him because I didn't want him to be worried. The situation was really confusing, and even more so as I knew that Jani could sense I really knew Something that he didn't want to know himself. Jani's defence forces were doing their best not to let anything "extra" slip into his consciousness. Jani was listening to himself.

A couple of days went by. We were touring the city like other tourists seeing the sights. I acted normally. As a matter of fact, I was relieved to be able to do something – anything – because then I didn't have to face myself, really face myself. I was aware of my self but I didn't want to face myself. I didn't want to face all my fears and the feelings they caused. The self was feeding or trying to feed me these fears continuously. By doing something, for example by walking, talking, looking, eating and listening I could direct my attention elsewhere. I managed to keep myself together and not fall apart. I was building – or rather the self was building – the weakly balanced, shaky foundation I already mentioned. I was going on an inner battle.

I felt weaker and weaker. I didn't have any appetite again and couldn't sleep well at night. For a few days I had had the strength to go around on foot but afterwards in the evening I was always totally exhausted. The restlessness could be seen physically too, my hands were literally shaking. I did everything in my power to keep myself together. The self didn't want to give in, not at all. The end was, however, near.

One day we were walking again in the centre of Sydney when I suddenly felt I could burst into tears at any moment. Anxiously I asked Jani to help me because I felt I had to lie down somewhere. I wanted to rest and listen to music because that seemed to calm me down. At this stage – or even earlier – many people would have resorted to medicines or some other numbing substance. I felt so uncomfortable that I could very well understand that somebody would not want to tolerate a feeling like that. But I didn't want to take any sedatives because I knew they would only cover that which I had to face anyway, sooner or later. I was by no means a heroine but I had the advantage of knowing what caused my suffering. I observed the sufferer and suffered. I couldn't handle that I knew. I couldn't handle that people around me went on living their normal lives and that I knew how things really were. The Truth was too much for myself. I was on the verge of despair. What if I can't stand myself? What if I lose it for real? What if I can't function normally any more? What if I just can't go on? What if I just break?

I began to be afraid of myself. A fear that I couldn't have even imagined before began to approach me.

I decided that I had to do something. I just couldn't go on with my crazy mind any longer. It had been leading me around all my life. It was the reason for my eternal feeling of insufficiency. It complained and demanded, wanted and accused. It reproached and subdued me. All my life it had ordered what I should do. It made me scared. I didn't want to suffer any longer, and I didn't want Jani to suffer either. My fearful restlessness was turning into hatred. I started to hate myself. The spectator began to hate the actor on the stage. I didn't want to listen to myself any more. I was up to my ears of myself! I wanted my mind to keep quiet just for one minute, even a couple of seconds, even just one second. I wanted to get rid of myself. I wanted to be in peace. I had had enough, just enough! I had to put an end to everything.

Suddenly I remembered the piece of paper the man had given me. I took it out and looked at the word written on it: "vipassana". I decided to find out what it meant, and I soon got to know that it was a form of meditation. I still didn't know what meditation really was but according to the information I found on the Internet I could participate in a ten-day free course. I also remembered the evening when the man had wanted to show me a surprise. He had invited me just to sit still with my eyes closed. I didn't then have the faintest idea what the man had wanted to show me but now I knew what the surprise was. I was watching it "from aside" all the time. The course had to have something to do with the surprise. The man had said that many people sit like that for days voluntarily. A cold shiver went down my spine. I knew now what I had to do. I knew I had to take part in the course because then I would be forced to just be. I read the rules of the course and noticed that there were no escapes. You couldn't do anything at all during the course, not even listen to music. I would be compelled just to be, and then forced to face my self. The fear beside me sneered and grew stronger and stronger. I wasn't at all sure whether I could face my self. Could I really get through it? I sighed deeply because I knew inside that I couldn't go on like this either. I couldn't keep escaping forever. If I couldn't tolerate my self at least I'd have a chance to go crazy in peace, and away from Jani's worried eyes.

We were supposed to fly to Auckland in New Zealand in a few days, so I looked on the net to see if they had any courses there. And yes! There was a suitable course beginning a day after our arrival in Auckland. As I didn't believe in coincidences anymore I applied right away.

I got a positive answer the next day. Soon the battle lay ahead. The fear that I was experiencing felt real; I was really afraid. I was afraid that I might really go mad or even die. I decided to send a message to my family and friends – it was time to say goodbye. I didn't phone anybody because talking on the phone would have been just too much for me. Even writing e-mail messages was difficult. I wept hysterically and tried to concentrate. I was really afraid I wouldn't see any of these dear people any more. But I had to leave everything – my whole life. There's no way I could explain how I felt. Many people have asked me afterwards why I went on that course, if I was so scared of going mad there. I just didn't have any other alternative any more. I had come to a crossroads and I knew which direction to take whether I liked it or not. I now know that many people stand at a similar crossroads for years. They know where to go but don't have the courage to continue the journey. Instead they stand still glancing furtively at the direction which they will have to take some day anyway. They know inside themselves that they are just putting off the decision to a later date, even if they themselves believe otherwise. They continue suffering without daring to take the first step. They don't understand that there is no choice. One can only push the decision a little further away.

I understood this clearly now. I didn't really want to be standing here at these crossroads, I wanted to be somewhere else, anywhere else. But there I was standing, terrified and alone. My journey had led me to the point of no return. I had been walking in the labyrinth long enough. There was only one decision, the decision that I would have to make sooner or later anyway.

In a couple of days I had already started the course. I had left everything behind – my belongings, my loved ones, my whole life. I had said goodbye to the man, the family and friends I loved. I had given up everything, literally everything. I was standing at the crossroads looking in the direction I should go. I had to continue my journey alone, completely alone. I couldn't take anything from my life with me, and there was nobody who could help. Guards started to gather on the road in front of me; my defense forces were getting ready for battle. The self didn't want me to continue and was going to do everything to prevent me from going on.

One of the guards was insufficiency. He was bent over from laughing and jeering at me mercilessly. Desire was standing beside him. She was girded with weapons which helped to keep me in her grip. On her belt hung bars of chocolate, bottles of alcohol, intimacy, all types of food, action, adventure and travelling, all kinds of experiences and so on. Next to desire was her twin sister need. She was also carrying weapons that looked even more powerful than her sister's: pictures of all the persons I loved were hanging like bandoliers around her neck – the pictures that I had just said goodbye to. This guard knew; I saw from her eyes that she knew. On the other side of desire was guilt. He was a big strong guy who looked like he loved his job. Brandishing his baton menacingly, he seemed to stand in front of my path, only so that he could flog shit-talkers like me. Next to him was the sense of responsibility. He had the Finnish flag on the front of his shirt. Then came worry, looking extremely familiar. He was so massive that he looked more like the Michelin-Man than a human being. There was a huge crowd of guards, an incredible number, and more came along all the time: suspicion, criticizing, judging, belittling, subduing, submission, sacrifice, shame, sorrow, failure, comparing, lying, owning, clinging, remorse, controlling, power, lust, humiliation, bitterness, hatred, envy, pride, reputation, honour, anxiety, restlessness, loneliness, despair... there was no end to be seen.

Suddenly my attention was drawn to a guard standing right at the front. He was clearly the leader, the boss who was responsible for the other guards. His eyes were full of fire and he was squeezing the baton in his hand so firmly that his knuckles were bleeding. There was something especially horrible about him, something indescribable, this something he knew about himself too. And I'm not only referring to his outer appearance, it was something even more horrible that was emanating from within him. I recognized the boss right away: he was fear. And not just any fear but the fear of all fears. The fear that trained all the other fears to serve himself. The fear that gave power to all the other fears. The fear that was the source of all the other fears. The fear which was called death. The fear of death was standing right in front of my eyes.

I looked at all the guards, the large crowd through which I knew it was impossible to move through. It was quite clear to me that they would all fight to the death. I knew that fear would greatly enjoy getting the chance to torture me. He would probably eat my body in front of all the others only to show everybody who the real winner was. The situation could very well have been amusing if I hadn't known I would die. How could I ever get through this impenetrable wall of defenses all by myself? The task was simply impossible. Nobody could understand. Nobody could understand why one would even want to try to go on from that point. I didn't even understand it myself. The attempt was doomed to fail but there was still something that urged me onwards. Something behind the defence forces – inside me – kept saying: "Come on, continue your journey, try." That Something is simply inexplicable.

So I took a step forward and stared hard at the crowd in front of me, shouting red faced, at the top of my voice: "All right, come on! Come on! Charge me! What are you waiting for?! I can't wait any longer! I'm ready! I'm ready to fight!!"

Like an avalanche the fear rolled over me, a fear beyond imagining. I was terrified. This I can't take anymore! I could not possibly face the feeling inside me. It had to lead to death. There was still something in me yelling: "No! No! I don't want to die! No! No! I want to live and exist. No! I don't want everything to end." Finally I understood that there was nothing to be done any more. I simply could not do anything anymore: Now I would die. I sank down to my knees surrendering completely. I had no strength to try any more. I had no strength to fight. Let death come. Let everything end. Let everything Be. And at that very moment the guards lowered their weapons – the road ahead was clear. All resistance was over. All attacking was over. All defending was over. All trying was over. All clinging was over. All need was over. All suffering was over. All that was left was Peace, deep lasting Peace.

PART THREE

Free from the shell

25

Taking responsibility

After the course, I wasn't afraid of myself any more; I wasn't afraid of fear. And because I wasn't afraid of fear, I wasn't afraid. After the course, there was nobody who was afraid. My self was dead. I understood that even the fear of death was only a feeling caused by a thought, perhaps the worst feeling ever but still only a feeling. No feeling that produces suffering lasts if you face it in the present moment. No feeling can take control if you face it in the present moment. The self cannot hold you in its grip if you face it in the present moment. Although I already knew before the course that I wasn't Sanna, my self still kept trying to fight back. So I developed a fear that seemed genuine. It was real to my self. I had the courage to face my worst fear thanks to the inner Voice because I trusted It enough. I trusted It more than my self. The new Ground on which I was standing seemed firm enough, and after the course I trusted It completely. There is no death; only the fear of death feels real.

The self always accepts in the end. Sooner or later it stops its fight. It surrenders and in doing so merges into Everything. The self vanishes and humbly returns back Home. There is nobody else. There is only everything that Is.

I wanted to face my self consciously because I knew who the source of my suffering was. I took full responsibility for my self. I didn't blame anybody else for my suffering. I knew that nobody else was responsible for my feelings. This may be a very difficult thing to accept. The self often wants to push the responsibility outside without realizing that it is outside itself. No one around you is responsible for your suffering – not your spouse, your children, your parents, your boss, your living environment, your illness or your whole world. You have to face everything you have developed and made yourself.

Taking responsibility is a big step forward. As long as you exist you are responsible. But it doesn't mean you should accuse yourself because there are no culprits. You just have to discover how things are, accept, and finally, surrender. Unconditional, neutral observation is an essentially important part in taking responsibility.

26

Forgiveness

I finished the previous chapter by saying that there are no culprits, but I too made myself feel guilty at first. When I understood who was responsible for my suffering the self took advantage of the situation and began to accuse itself. The spectator began to accuse the main actor. By making accusations, I directed the hatred to my self. The self is cunning. It tried to preserve its own existence – and succeeded for a while – by accusing itself. But I noticed it. I noticed the desperate attempt of the self to survive, and when I became aware of this I felt strong compassion towards my self. The self didn't understand what the ramifications of its existence were; it just wanted to stay alive. It was innocent. I was ready to forgive. I was ready to forgive my self. I took my self in my Lap like an innocent child and filled it with Love. I Loved my self. And because I Loved my self I couldn't help but Love everything else too. My forgiveness was so all-inclusive that my self melted down. I melted into a Love I couldn't have dreamed of. All suffering vanished completely. Tears of Joy rolled down my cheeks. I had returned Home. I was Free and Happy.

I can't even begin to describe how important forgiving is. Forgiving is the shortest road to the Destination. You can't find the way Home until you are able to forgive everybody and everything. Everything that's happened in your life has happened so that you could forgive. By forgiving, you can leave the past behind. The past disperses and all that's left is Now. You can take the sack from your shoulders and look through it. You can take all your memories and put them on the table in front of you, and forgive everybody and everything you consider guilty. By forgiving, the sack will be left permanently on the ground. By forgiving, you can fly. By forgiving, you are Free to recognize what you really Are.

Many people stay in a trap of guilt. The self is an expert in making use of guilt; it can work it up into many different forms. Hatred and pity are two splendid examples of this. Nobody can hate without guilt. By hating, the self accuses the object it has judged itself. By hating, the self feeds itself. In addition to hatred, the self also desires pity. It loves to bathe in self-pity and make complaints about everything imaginable. By pitying itself or some other object it is immersed in guilt. Love never pities or hates. Love can do nothing else but Love.

Love never criticizes or accuses. Love never judges anyone or anything. For this reason, Love doesn't forgive either. Love can't forgive because Love knows there is nothing to forgive. There are no culprits. And because there are no culprits there isn't anyone or anything that could be blamed. Without guilt there is nothing to forgive. Only a person who has judged – in other words played a game made by themselves – can forgive. Love feels no guilt – Love doesn't even know what guilt is. Love only knows Itself.

You are walking in the labyrinth of your own will. Love is Free. You can do whatever you want. Love doesn't walk in a labyrinth or play any game, but you can walk and play if you want to. When you don't want to suffer anymore and don't want anyone else to suffer either, you are ready to forgive. You are ready to forgive your self.

27

Honesty

During the course I also came to understand the meaning of honesty. When I use the word honesty I'm talking about the open acceptance of your own truth – the truth that is true to you. When you are honest you do not try to vary your truth. When you are honest you have the courage to look the truth in the eyes. Honesty is of utmost importance because it is the road to Freedom; when you are honest you aren't afraid, and when you aren't afraid, you don't suffer.

The self lives with the help of fear. The self is the fear. The self does not dare to look the Truth in the eye. It lies in order to preserve its existence. By lying it takes advantage of your truth. It covers and avoids the truth. The self does whatever it takes to prevent you from being honest.

For your self the truth changes constantly. Your truth can change daily or at least over the years. How often this happens makes no difference. Even the change itself is of no importance. You can still be honest. You can be honest about your truth at this particular moment, but when you know the Truth, the Truth no longer changes.

Honesty is closely connected with trust, and through trust, with the inner Voice. Before you have the courage to trust in Life, you are afraid to be honest. The self never trusts anything else but itself, and therefore it is natural for it to lie. It invents all kinds of reasons and ways for you not to be honest. It tries to lead you deeper and deeper into the illusion of mind, not out of it. The inner Voice however is always honest. It doesn't lie and It knows what you really want. The inner Voice always leads you towards Love. That is why the self doesn't want you to listen to It. The self does everything in its power to make you not do what the inner Voice invites you to do. The self constantly invents all kinds of distortions to cover the inner Voice, and lying is one of its most powerful means.

The self makes use of lying very skillfully. In addition to conscious lying, it also wants you to sacrifice yourself. Sacrificing oneself is also a form of lying because then you are not doing what you really want to do. By sacrificing yourself you do what the self wants you to do, that is, what you believe it is best to do. Society often regards sacrificing oneself as an admirable characteristic – or at least that's what the self wants you to believe because sacrifice helps the self preserve its existence.

The inner Voice never wants you to do anything other than what you really want to do. By listening to the inner Voice you always do what you Love doing. This might sound confusing. Why would one do things that one really doesn't want to? On the other hand, you might just as well ask why one listens to oneself in the first place or why one wants to suffer. The self makes up incredible reasons for why listening to the inner Voice is to no avail. It points to ideas and actions that it considers correct and of course has developed itself, and feeds you with an enormous amount of suspicion and accusation. It makes you feel guilty and afraid of the judgements of others. It makes you feel afraid of itself. In other words, if doubts and other troublesome obstacles are not enough, it resorts to its best weapon. Fear is always the mightiest of its shields and the best means to make you back up.

The self always takes advantage of lying to protect something. It really makes you believe that you can protect something if you lie. It doesn't matter what kind of form the object that needs protection is, because in the end it is always just the self's own need to protect itself. By lying it lures you deeper into the labyrinth. By lying you might believe you will be protected against something that threatens you. Therefore it is important that you ask yourself: What is it that I am trying to be protected against? What am I trying to cover? What am I trying to defend? Why don't I have the courage to be honest? Why don't I dare listen to my inner Voice?

Honesty is connected with responsibility. You are responsible for your own decisions. You are responsible, whether you listen to your inner Voice or your self. You are responsible for your honesty. Nobody else can take responsibility for your honesty because nobody else knows your truth. You can be honest only to your own truth. By lying, you are only playing the game you have made up yourself, the game that only takes you deeper into the labyrinth. At the Destination, there is nobody who lies – that is totally impossible. At the Destination, there is nobody who tries to cover or vary the Truth. At the Destination, there is nobody in need of protection. At the Destination, there is nobody to be afraid.

28

Thankfulness

After the course, I felt peaceful, or rather all that was left was Peace. I'm still telling the story in the first person although there isn't any person in Me anymore who could identify herself with the actor or the spectator. After the course, there was nobody here anymore. I didn't play a part any more, consciously or unconsciously. Sanna was only a shell, a stage prop that others used in their own plays. If Sanna would have still performed in the play, she would have performed a role she didn't know, a role that was recreated every moment, a role that had no past or future, a role that couldn't be played according to any model or idea, a role that was not present.

I described earlier how I took myself in My Lap like an innocent child and how I merged into a Love that I couldn't even have imagined. This self in My Lap, or rather the faint shadow that was left of it – a memory vanishing into the air like smoke – raised its head now and then, but it didn't take control anymore. It was content just to take a look around after which I took it tenderly into My Lap again. It didn't even want to jump off. It felt no need to go its own way anymore. Sometimes it just looked around as if searching for something and even tried to speak occasionally, but lost interest the moment it saw where it Was. The Lap of Love was more than enough for it; it was Home again and now wanted just to bask in Love.

The shadow of the self and its existence is by no means an easy thing to describe because I Know it doesn't exist. Yet it still seems like there is something here, something that I Am not. Just like Sanna still seems to be here, the shadow of the self seems to be here too.

After the course I was full of Love, I Is Love. The Foundation I was now standing on was strong and reliable. I knew that It could never break beneath me, nor fail me – it was totally impossible. The Foundation was everything that Is. The Peace that could only be felt in the background before the course was on me now: I Was in It. The storm had subsided and the sky was bright and clear. I Was Happy.

Jani noticed the change immediately and was very glad and relieved for me. The course had lasted for ten days, during which time Jani had been in Auckland and the vicinity. After some initial doubts, he had trusted my decision to participate in the course. He understood very well that I needed time just to be. Now the course was over and we could continue our journey. Jani had rented us a new well-functioning camper van and couldn't wait to see the sights of New Zealand. He suggested that we first drive towards Cape Reinga, the northernmost tip of New Zealand. That plan suited me just fine. Everything suited me just fine. I would have been ready to go north, south, east or west, anywhere, or even to stay in Auckland. Everything was fine. Everything interested me.

I sent a message home to my family and friends, explaining that everything was fine, more than fine, and nobody needed to worry. I wasn't a member of any vipassana-sect and didn't fanatically practice anything – nothing at all. I did say a few words about the course to many people and recommended it to everybody. I've sometimes been asked how I had the courage to talk about everything so thoroughly and openly, but for me it had been quite clear. It was so evident that there were no doubts whatsoever. I was open and totally fearless. I didn't feel ashamed and I didn't have a thought, of what others thought of me. To me it seemed quite natural to tell others about everything I had found out. Love can do nothing but Love. It winks kindly at everybody and asks: "Do you want to stop suffering too?" or: "Do you want to get out of the labyrinth too?" Some of the passers-by may shake their heads in wonder and go on their way. Others stop to listen for more. Love is content with anything. It is just available. It announces Joyfully that It is there.

We spent nearly two months in New Zealand. We drove from one place to another and saw all kinds of beauty. We spent the night wherever we saw fit – generally on a magnificent beach. We had no fixed plan but stopped and went on every time we felt like it. Travelling was leisurely and effortless. Life took care of everything for us and we had only to enjoy it all. I trusted Life completely. I knew I was exactly where I was supposed to be in each moment. The actor moved and performed the role on the stage just as it was supposed to. I was grateful for everything I received and just as gratefully shared it with others. I gave to Myself and received from Myself. The Love Loved Itself. Our trip was full of lovely surprises. As I myself had stepped aside and I Myself had come out of the shell, Something else planned my days, and this Something knew exactly what It was doing. My days were filled with Joy. It emerged out of the sea of Peace, jumping high like a dolphin. It laughed and Loved.

Our tour of New Zealand ended in Christchurch. Although the time in New Zealand had been wonderful, I didn't feel sad when it ended. I knew that the real Journey didn't end in New Zealand, It would go on forever: the environment changed but the Journey continued. I knew that Life was eternal, not this reality, this dream, but Life Itself. Weather conditions change but the Sky stays the same.

After the course I was very Thankful. I had been thankful for life for years but now the feeling was deeper. There wasn't anybody anymore who could have been thankful, it was just Thankfulness that was left. Thankfulness is a natural state – if it can be called a state – of What you really Are. It wells forth naturally from Somewhere and returns Somewhere. Thankfulness doesn't carry the burden of guilt. It doesn't feel it owes anyone anything and It doesn't feel ill at ease for anything that It's been given. It has no need to please anybody either. Thankfulness is the natural result of what you Are when you give and receive from Yourself. It's impossible not to be Thankful when you know what you really Are.

Thankfulness is a natural reaction when you know you are enough, when you feel you don't lack anything. All that the false self knows of Thankfulness is just its shadow, and it therefore wants to own and have more and more of what gave rise to that feeling. The self regards thankfulness only as a feeling and as a need that it can fulfill from some specific target. The self bases thankfulness on 'because of' and 'if you'. It cannot be grateful without guilt. The self always feels it owes something when it receives something. It is grateful because it is able to patch up the feeling of lack temporarily but knows at the same time that the patch is only borrowed and must be returned as soon as possible. The self plays a game with itself. It is called "Thank you for giving up and sacrificing yourself, I do the same thing myself." This game is based on guilt. The self can never feel permanently Thankful because it stands in the way of Thankfulness itself.

Thankfulness leads you to the Destination; it is like a road sign that shows you the way. Every time you feel grateful, you are near your destination, the destination that is always now, in this moment. It is impossible to feel thankful when you are suffering, and that is usually the reason why the self cannot recognize thankfulness. The self wants you to suffer rather than be thankful and at the same time happy. Thankfulness and happiness are too close to your real Being and therefore it is important that you recognize; what is it in you that is not thankful and what is it in you that feels ill at ease when you give and receive something?

29

The inner Power

From Christchurch we flew back to Sydney, Australia, after which we continued our journey to Bali, Indonesia. We had already booked all the flights before Christmas and had planned to stay in Bali for nearly a month, after which we would return to Finland via Bangkok.

Bali turned out to be a marvellous place and time just flew past surfing (read: drowning), touring and reading. I hadn't read anything after the course but now the situation had changed. Life had thrown a book on the power of thought into my hands, a book a friend of mine had recommended to me. I decided to read it.

I already knew that I wasn't my thoughts, that is my mind, neither was I my body. That led me to ponder why thoughts and the body actually existed after all. The shadow of the self woke up and appeared to still be here although I wasn't here Myself anymore. This question didn't, however, bother me because nothing bothered me anymore – It just appeared and I looked at it with interest. I understood that the body and all the thoughts were in Me, in other words in Mind. So, the Mind is not in the body, the body is in the Mind. What I Am includes everything: I Am everywhere. I am not in the mind, in the labyrinth, but in the Mind, everywhere and in everything. The shadow of my self still seemed to be here forming thoughts, and the question had sprung up from these thoughts. I Myself never ask anything because I don't have anything to ask. All questions arise from the little self. The little self asks itself the questions it has itself formed. Questions are a way to preserve its existence. The self desires contemplation and analysis. It uses problems and riddles as a means of surviving.

The book on the power of thought was fun and interesting: according to it, life is like a mail-order catalogue and all the orders are made by thinking. The book was full of advice and instructions on how the labyrinth can be made a more beautiful and attractive place. I wasn't interested anymore in what the labyrinth looked like or what it felt like to be there. The book aroused my interest only because it helped me to understand how the labyrinth is formed and how I could help other people to get out of it. The labyrinth may seem a beautiful and wonderful place at times, but it is still only a labyrinth. You can't understand – the self doesn't understand – that you can't be totally Free and Happy until you get out of it.

What I Am and what you Are too creates all the time, constantly and incessantly. Creating always happens in this moment - now - because everything happens in this moment. Creating could be called your birth right because it is, has always been and will always be in you. You create with thoughts all the time, even unconsciously. You yourself build your life constantly with thoughts. With the help of thoughts everything around you takes shape: you yourself are only a thought as well.

You create without pause, and when you identify yourself with your self, you create yourself. Then the self forms appropriate thoughts and creates what it wants. When you know what you really Are, it is Love that creates. Then Love creates using Thoughts. You Are a Thought. It is up to you which one creates, your self or You Yourself. If you let the little self lead you, you create what the self wants, but if you let Love lead you, you create only what you Love. The self doesn't Love you. It only wants to create for itself, even if that brings you suffering, whereas Love Loves you and wants you to create only what you Love. Love always wants what is best for you and at the same time what is best for everybody for there is no one else. Love wants you to be Happy.

The self only wants what's best for itself and for those who it feels are a part of it. The self's idea of what is best leads always to suffering. You suffer and others suffer. The self doesn't want you to be Happy – its only purpose is to preserve its existence.

You have an incredible Power inside you and with the help of this Power you can create whatever you want – there are no limits. It depends on you, whether you create using thoughts or Thoughts. When you create using little thoughts it is your self that creates and this self also sets limits to what you can create. When you create using Thoughts you create Yourself and there are no limits whatsoever. This means that there is a Power inside you that makes everything possible, literally everything. This Power could perhaps be compared to air (or oxygen): just like air makes your existence possible, the Power makes Your Existence possible. However the Power is not – just like air isn't – responsible for your decisions; it just makes everything possible. With your free will you can create whatever you want.

The little self generally uses this Power very destructively. It has to attack and defend in order to be able to exist. It uses thoughts only for the benefit of itself and therefore whatever it creates has a destructive effect on the body it considers its slave (your body), and on everything else around it. The self is the root of all suffering. There is no other hell than the extreme need of the self to exist. The thoughts of the self that produce suffering creates suffering.

Love instead creates in a completely different way. Its Thoughts don't even know what suffering means. Love is so far from suffering that It has simply never even faced it at all. Only the self knows what suffering is. When Love creates, Its impact is reflected everywhere and in everything, including the body. Love has no limits, It is in everybody and in everything. Love affects in the opposite way than the self. Love heals and diminishes suffering. Love Loves everybody and everything, Love Loves Itself.

Love is not part of the dream, the reality that the self calls life. The dream is born from the self. Love Is, however, behind the dream because It is everywhere and in everything. When you wake up from the dream, a hole is made and Love shines into the dream through this hole. A Ray of Sun reaches the labyrinth and this Ray creates with Thoughts. These Thoughts are gentle and understanding, certain and full of Love. They emanate Joy and Happiness. They are encouraging and do not insult or belittle. The Thoughts of Love unite, they don't separate. They don't attack, defend or judge. The Thoughts of Love are full of Peace. When you create using these Thoughts creation is like celebration – effortless and full of Joy.

I noticed a change in my thinking. I thought no more according to the old model. I had considerably fewer Thoughts than before, and They always appeared spontaneously, in this moment. The new Thoughts were also clearly bright, not vague or messy. The shadow of the self still went on creating too, but it had no effect on Me anymore. The thoughts of the self just came and went. I didn't cling to them, neither did I prevent them from appearing, for there was nobody that could cling to or prevent them from coming. I had no need to react to the thoughts of the self, however. I reacted quite naturally to the new Thoughts.

The inner Voice digs a hole in the dream. All you need do is listen to It. The inner Voice changes your thoughts into Thoughts. The more you listen to the inner Voice, the more your creations change. The inner Voice knows how to use the Power in you. If you let It, the inner Voice will guide you until you know what you Are. Your journey towards Love can begin. When you reach the Destination you won't listen to any separate voice anymore for then there will be nobody who listens. At the Destination, there is only a Voice, One Voice. At the Destination, there is nothing else but Love.

The idea of Power, and particularly the idea of the power of thought, might sound suspicious to you. If that is the case, it is worth while asking yourself who it is that suspects. Only the self imagines that it is just an insignificant body who owns insignificant thoughts. Only the self accuses something outside itself for its experiences. Only the self is unwilling to bear the responsibility for its creations.

Although the thoughts of the self are destructive they can never destroy You. The self can destroy your body and fill your mind with suffering-producing thoughts, but it can never harm what you really Are.

30

A relationship — a means of the self to preserve its existence

A few days before we left Bali for Bangkok Jani and I talked about our return to Finland. We both knew already what was going to happen but now it was time to talk about it aloud. We decided to break up. I had no need for a relationship anymore, and Jani too wanted some time to be alone. The shadow of the self in my Lap woke up again – I felt melancholy and sad. These feelings didn't, however, have any effect on Me; they were like passing clouds. As I already mentioned, there was nobody in Me anymore who would cling to or prevent the clouds from coming. The clouds just appeared in the Sky and soon disappeared. I Loved Jani and wanted him to be Happy. Saying this I mean that I Loved Myself, the Love Loved Itself. The Love Loved Love. And this Love is so all-inclusive that It literally melted the clouds away from the Sky.

The love that the self calls love can be preserved only with the help of fear. Fear makes you need something. And a couples relationship, like all other relationships, provides this something. With the help of this something the self tries – and temporarily succeeds – to cover the fear. In a relationship the self offers and gives you what you feel you need. This need can take any form. It can mean security, status, entertainment, intimacy or togetherness that saves you from loneliness. No matter what the relationship gives you, its ultimate purpose is to hide the fear. The self is cunning – it wants you to be afraid but doesn't want you to face the fear. When a couple relationship, or any other kind of relationship, for example, a relation to a child, friend, or pet ends for some reason, the fear rises to the surface. The fear arises right in front of you. But the self doesn't want you to face this fear and because of that it quickly clings to the feeling. By clinging it manages to keep the feeling to itself. Practically speaking, this means that you feel fear and all the other feelings born from it.

Fear gives rise to a great number of different feelings. Sorrow and nostalgia are two examples of them. They are the result of giving up. When the relationship is over there is nothing that covers the feeling of lack. When the feeling of lack rises to the surface you also feel lonely.

In addition to loneliness, sorrow and nostalgia, hatred and bitterness might also arise. Hatred is born out of guilt – which again is born out of fear – and through that a need to judge. You may feel angry because you think you have been betrayed. You feel betrayed because you have not Loved, you have sacrificed. And because you have done so, you want others to sacrifice too. You need an object you can blame for your sacrificing, because if you hadn't made sacrifices you wouldn't have any reason to judge. By hating and at the same time judging the other, you avoid looking at yourself. The self generally wants to accuse somebody outside; it wants to project its feelings outside itself although it is an outsider itself as well. It doesn't want to see things as they are. It doesn't want to take responsibility.

Your need – the need of your little self – to preserve a need drives you to sacrifice yourself. By doing so you are able to keep the need, in other words the object you need. This also means that you are lying. By sacrificing, you actually do something you don't really want to do: the need has driven you to make sacrifices and at the same time to do something that you really don't want to do. This strategy developed by the self is based on guilt and in the end always pushes you to judge others. The self is inconceivably cunning in planning strategies.

Fear is also the cause of restlessness, anxiety and depression. All these are feelings that very easily become entangled to make a big lump. This lump can grow so big that it may be impossible to carry it any more. It swells and swells because of the guilt. Guilt keeps all the feelings lumped together; it is the strongest glue that can ever be found on the market. This lump that has originated in fear causes a lot of suffering to the carrier and appears as both mental and physical symptoms. One may, for example, become more and more deeply depressed, which can lead right down to self-destruction. A self-destructive person has no strength to do anything and the sheer exhaustion may ultimately drive the individual to suicide. Of course, self destructiveness doesn't always end with the destruction of the body; more commonly symptoms appear as constant tiredness, despondency, burn-out, different kinds of panic disorders or general restlessness.

Mental burdens always affects the body. In the body, the burden might appear as slight symptoms, such as gaining or losing weight, or stronger symptoms such as various kinds of tumours and other illnesses. All physical symptoms as well as mental illnesses originate in the self. As I have already emphasized in various ways, the self doesn't care for consequences – its only aim is to preserve its own existence. For this reason the only way to get rid of the burden is to face it. Only by laying the sack down, by examining it without judgement, and by forgiving everyone and everything can you break Free. Only by Loving yourself will the suffering end.

Different relationships are one of the most effective means by which the self preserves its existence. This is the reason why it is so important to discover what it is in you that wants to hold on to a certain relationship. What is it in you that hates and feels bitter? What accuses and judges? What grieves and is afraid of being alone?

When You Love, the result can never be hatred or bitterness, nor sadness, melancholy or disappointment, and there is no need to lie. This is why you can never end up feeling lonely, restless, anxious or depressed. Then there is no guilt or fear. There is only Love – then Love Loves Itself.

When there is Love, there is no need to hold on to anything. There is no need to make agreements, nor are there predetermined models of action. Then nobody sacrifices anything and nobody is guilty of anything. Then there is nothing to judge and no need to lie. Then there is no suffering. Then Love is Alone. Then Love only Loves.

31

The self, the source of all symptoms

The last days in Bali went by quickly, and we soon found ourselves in Bangkok, Thailand. We had begun our journey from this city and wanted to end it there too. The journey would soon be over – like everything that appears in the dream sooner or later is.

After a couple of days we left the bustling crowds of Bangkok behind and were on a plane again. This time our destination was Finland. I felt calm and peaceful. Another way of saying this is that my role character was sitting contentedly on the seat looking through the window watching the clouds passing by. The journey that had lasted a year and a half was over, and the story of Sanna had a few new turns. I had made my dream come true and listened to the inner Voice without knowing it – I had done what I really Loved. I hadn't had the faintest idea Where the Instinct would lead me. I was, however, very Grateful for It. The story of Sanna still seemed to continue but it didn't touch Me in any way anymore.

My parents were at the airport waiting for me when we arrived in Finland. I was extremely happy – my role character was jumping up and down with excitement. In front of me stood two very meaningful characters in my performance. But when I Looked at them both I only Saw Myself. How wonderful I was! After a lot of hugging we went to my parents' place. Later on I met my sisters and their families too: more actors with important roles in my play. There was a lot of hugging and laughing again – oh, how I Loved Myself! Soon I saw my friends too and the same thing repeated itself – so much Love, oh, so much Love! Later on, when I was walking in the centre of Helsinki, I could have hugged every passer-by. I Loved Myself so much, oh, how I Loved Myself. I Was full of Love and so Happy.

At the beginning, my family and friends probably understood my state of mind as one who had just returned home to loved ones from a long journey. But after a time, when there was no change, I began to notice confused, even worried looks around me. I had just separated from the man I loved very much. I had no apartment of my own or job to go back too. I couldn't possibly be alright. There must be some symptoms of anxiety caused by the separation, maybe even of trauma. I must have some kind of culture shock, or maybe I was just hiding a thirty-something crisis.

After returning to Finland I still felt that it was almost impossible for me to express in words what had happened. I just invited everybody to read the book I had mentioned and to listen to the Instinct. I also encouraged everybody to do what they really Loved doing, and kept repeating like a parrot that everything Is Love. This lack of capacity for oral expression pushed me to search for more information because I also wanted to understand for myself what it was that I knew. In My Lap, the shadow of my self was wondering why it was sitting there surrounded by Love. My role character began to attract various kinds of books and other sources of information. I read several spiritual books during the next few months and acquainted myself with different religions. Furthermore, science interested me and I soon understood that everybody was actually searching for the same Thing, talking about the same Thing. I also noticed what kind of net had been formed around It without my knowing.

I spent a lot of time at my parents' summer cottage, I practically lived there. I had returned to Finland in late May when the spring was in full bloom. The promising scent of summer was spreading all over and nature was a dazzling green. The days went by and I drifted with them. I spent a lot of time with my family and friends. I saw Jani too, a couple of times. I swam in the lake and bathed in the sauna. The summer was beautiful and warm, the sun was shining and in the north there was even twenty-four hours of daylight.

Besides reading books, I also plunged deeper into music and art; all of a sudden, everything was so beautiful and fascinating. The power of Loves' creation silenced my role character. I Myself was so amazingly skillful. Creation could be seen everywhere. I Saw everything in a completely new way – the point of view had changed from the self to Love. I noticed how Love kept creating for everyone and everything. Love took everything into account and Thought of the Whole, not only the individual. Love couldn't create any other way. Love only created more Love. Love just expanded and expanded. Love created for Itself. I also noticed clearly how the self created: it created only for itself and only had in mind what was best for itself and those belonging to it. This "best for the self" was like a sick joke. In the end the creations of the self couldn't bring joy even to the individual in question. In the end they always led to suffering: the individual suffered and everybody around suffered.

This change of view had an effect on my environment but also on the experiences of my role character. There was no need to attempt anything any more, events took their own course. I just Loved. All actions were effortless and full of Love. I could use physical exercise as an example of this: Love gave exercising a totally new starting point. I stopped torturing myself by jogging and lifting weights to exhaustion. There was nobody left who should exercise, lose weight or be worried about their appearance. There was nobody left who should move because of guilt. All that was left was the sheer Joy of moving and exercising. I Loved doing sports and other exercises. I roller-skated, did yoga and went for walks for the sheer Joy of it. I'm now talking of yoga merely as a form of exercise because I didn't have a need to get anywhere or maintain anything by doing yoga. I had learned a series of yoga asanas which I had already been doing during our journey, and that was what I still went on doing. Nevertheless, I had never really thought deeply what the purpose of yoga was; for me it had simply been a way to move, stretch your limbs and calm the mind. It was only after I had returned to Finland that I found out what the ultimate purpose of yoga is. Nowadays I can say that nobody needs to do yoga in order to know what one really Is. It is true that yoga soothes the mind and improves mental and physical balance. But the balance created and maintained by practising yoga is, however, just as frail as any built by the self. In the end no balance built by the self can last.

The self builds a balance with the help of yoga, for instance, by removing blockages that have collected in the body and by working the energy moving in the body. The self always concentrates on the body and blames the body willingly for its problems. The self tries, and may occasionally succeed temporarily, to ease the symptoms it has caused. Doing yoga improves your feeling temporarily but as long as the source of the symptoms is unknown, they keep returning. The self wants to concentrate on removing the symptoms but doesn't want to find the source of them.

I noticed that this need to remove symptoms could clearly be seen in western medicine too. When the self falls ill, it wants to recover and be healthy. The self wants to get rid of the symptoms which means that it wants to get rid of both the illness and the symptoms caused by the illness. It is content when the symptoms are removed or at least hidden. The self doesn't want you to understand that although the illness and the symptoms it causes disappear temporarily, they will soon reappear either in the same or a different form. As long as the original source of all the symptoms – which at the same time is the original source of all suffering – is not revealed to you, your mind – and through that your body – will react with symptoms. Practically, this means that you can ease symptoms by taking medicines or using different kinds of healing methods. You can talk to a psychologist for years and examine your story from a thousand different points of view. You can analyze your symptoms no end, but as long as you don't know what causes them you will continue suffering.

If you already know what causes all your symptoms I encourage you to just let them be. You don't have to do anything to them. When there is nobody who develops symptoms, holds on to them or tries to cover them, they disappear. This doesn't mean that you shouldn't tend to the symptoms and the suffering. There is no harm in going to see a psychologist or taking medicines. However, the most important thing is that you discover the source of the symptoms and don't let it have power in you. Love heals everything if you give It a chance.

All symptoms are only caused by a lack of Love. Another way of saying this is that there is someone in you that blocks Love. You don't have to go looking for health and Love, you only have to clear away all the obstacles in their way. The same goes for balance and peace of mind. You don't have to look for or maintain balance and peace of mind, you only have to discover why they are not possible for you. Love cannot enter if you block Its way yourself.

When there are no illnesses and generally no suffering anymore, all that is left is what Is. As long as there is someone in you that is ill and suffers, you don't know what you really Are. You may feel pain in your body but when you know what you Are you also know that you are not your body.

The self causes symptoms in many different ways. I, for example, had them with eating. I felt guilty when I ate, particularly after puberty. I didn't like my body and this was reflected in my eating habits. I tried to control myself through eating and exercising. There were periods when I watched my eating habits fanatically. This continuous control caused by the self led to temporary binges because I wanted to let go, even for a moment. After these attacks, I of course felt guilty, and the guilt made me exercise. A couple of times I even made myself vomit. I was developing bulimia. My attitude towards food had originated from my self, and I enjoyed eating only if I thought I had earned it. This usually meant that I had already done some exercise or I knew I would do some soon after eating. The self had developed a splendid strategy to preserve its existence. This strategy was, however, painful and caused suffering. The self's need to control everything often leads to the need to let go. And the need to let go also appears as excessive drinking, obsessive exercising, drug addiction and the continuous need to buy things, among numerous other examples.

After the course, my eating habits changed because there was no-body in Me anymore who wanted to control things or felt guilty. I had no need to let go anymore – I Was Free. There was nobody in Me who hated her body or felt the need to earn the food. Generally speaking, I didn't hate anything nor have to earn anything any more. I Loved Myself, so I Loved eating too. This doesn't mean that I started stuffing food whenever possible. Food wasn't my life. My role character ate everything gratefully and enjoyed what Life had to offer. There was no need to stuff or fast. The body needed food and my role character enjoyed eating. Even today I don't follow any particular diet, and there are no forbidden foodstuffs for me. My eating is free, I Am Free.

32

All but Love
comes and goes

The summer went by and it was soon autumn. The colours of the scenery changed from green to all the wonderful colours of autumn. The evenings grew darker and the fresh autumn wind played often with the fallen leaves on the ground. The general atmosphere changed in the whole country: for most people everyday routines had started again. The summer holidays were over and the winter lay ahead. I was still floating on – the Stream carried my role character. Nothing attracted me particularly. After Jani and I had separated, we had divided our bank savings in Finland between us, and I had enough money to live on. I didn't have to go to work immediately and I didn't have any need to save more money. As I look back at the situation now, it seems that Life allowed me to have a moment's rest. The shadow of my self in my Lap started to calm down. I just was – without any aims or goals. My role character didn't know what to do because no role attracted her. There was nothing to be done, owned, or achieved. I was Happy and very contented, without any particular reason. As I already mentioned, I just Loved. I Loved everybody and everything around me. I Was Love and I Loved Myself.

My role character constantly attracted interesting books and I read a lot. In fact, I had never before read as much as I did then. The world of books fascinated me more and more. Love expressed Itself in so many ways. Little by little, I was able to form some kind of picture of what had happened to me. And as I grew more skillful in using words, my enthusiasm to express my experiences grew too. Gradually there started to form Thoughts in front of me, in other words directional meanings about That which cannot be spoken about directly. These Thoughts were still in their infancy, but they began to take shape.

One day Life suggested through Jani that I should write a book: that is, I Myself suggested to Myself that I should write a book. I didn't See persons anymore, I only saw Myself. To me everything is part of Life, I Am Life. Hearing this suggestion, my role character burst out laughing because the idea was amusing in many ways. Sanna would have never written a book. Sitting in front of a computer voluntarily for hours was simply way too absurd an idea. Sanna had never dreamed of becoming a writer. There was a time in my younger days when my role character had been interested in writing but when it had become joyless and serious the interest had stopped. I didn't think I could write. Now the situation was different. I got excited about writing and I knew I could do anything. I didn't have the limits that my self had set before. I was eager to write the book because it would give Me a splendid opportunity to express what I knew.

For months and months I just wrote and wrote. I wrote many different versions before the text was in the form you are now reading. My role character sat in front of the computer for hundreds of hours brimming with enthusiasm. I Love writing.

During the writing process, Sanna's story took new twists and turns too. My role character met many new people who were walking in the labyrinth. Life organised situations that could sometimes be very surprising. Every moment brought something new. The conversations I had with my old and new friends (every person is my friend) helped to forward the writing process. Their desire to know urged Me to write. On the basis of these conversations, I was able to build the text into the form it is now. I also knew that many others would be drawn to this book. I simply wouldn't have written this book if you didn't want to consciously or unconsciously remember Yourself. I wouldn't have written this book if you weren't now holding it in your hands. Love calls to you. I'm Happy for you.

This book is exactly how it is supposed to be. I'm Glad that you have read it. There's still some more text left but it will soon be finished. This book will end, like everything in this dream sooner or later will. Only Love abides for It Is. I Love You.

Visit Sannas' website

www.freedomfromtheshell.com

If you would like to contact her directly email

sanna@freedomfromtheshell.com

www.ingramcontent.com/pod-product-compliance
Lightning Source LLC
Chambersburg PA
CBHW020919160726
47993CB00005B/2041